The Stuff of Life: Ancient Inspiration for Sustainable Living

The Stuff of Life: Ancient Inspiration for Sustainable Living

María Correas-Amador

PRESS

Published by Vulpine Press in the United Kingdom in 2022

ISBN: 978-1-83919-449-8

www.vulpine-press.com

To my father, who learnt tirelessly his whole life.

Contents

Foreword

I have been guiding scores of excited visitors through the ancient Egypt galleries at Spain's National Archaeology Museum for a number of years. Although a modest collection compared to other European capitals, it showcases all kinds of objects big and small, from sarcophagi to amulets. Visitor expectations are generally high, and they never leave disappointed: people love the mystery, the glamour and the majestic halo that wraps around all things Egyptian. Most of them book themselves into the tour to hear about powerful pharaohs, lavishly adorned mummies and capricious deities, and they return home satisfied having stood in front of jewels, gilded coffins and statuettes that confirm everything they imagined Egypt to be.

It makes me happy to say that what they are not usually prepared for, is to stand in front of a glass cabinet containing a loaf of bread or a pair of papyrus-woven sandals. These daily objects seem, somehow, too mundane to have been preserved for thousands of years, only for us to realise that we have an identical pair of flip-flops made of plastic. People's common reaction to these items is 'Wow, I never knew this existed', or 'How can this object possibly have survived for millennia?'. There is an easy answer for this last question, and it is Egypt's historical environmental conditions. Dryness has helped preserve many organic objects that otherwise would have rotted away. The first comment, though, should make archaeologists specialised in Egypt reflect on what we are doing wrong. Why are most people not aware of the wealth of baskets, food or linen tunics archaeologists have uncovered in Egypt? And why do they know all about Tutankhamen's mask or Nefertiti's bust? Clearly, the fact that these materials are perishable is no excuse. We cannot expect people to have a broad perspective of ancient cultures if we treat some objects as 'second class'. This book wants to end that biased view of ancient Egypt. The wealth of down-to-earth objects you will find in its pages opens a window into the lives of ancient Egyptian people, lives that had far more in common with ours than the pharaohs' ever could. These objects, as well as others from various cultures across the globe, will truly guide us through a journey that will connect our past with our present.

But there is a further dimension to that connection. The fact that these organic items are fantastically preserved also prompts us to reflect on the things that we produce, use and refuse. In a world where we increasingly realise our rate of consumption is not sustainable, they offer us a broader perspective, one through which we come to realise, for example, that the use of plastic is almost anecdotal in historical terms, even though we now feel like it has always been a part of our lives. By spotting their enduring traces in other modern cultures, we will learn what has made them survive for millennia. Furthermore, we will realise how important it is to preserve the (fundamentally oral) traditions that surround their production and that are rapidly disappearing. Unfortunately, in some cases, they are already gone.

So how is this book structured?

Some time ago, while researching breastfeeding in ancient Egypt, I came across some spells that talked about the deceased being born again as a baby that needing nurturing. It is a concept that feels natural in a way, as being elderly is returning to being like a baby in many tender ways. For the Egyptians, birth and rebirth were akin.

If we think of organic objects in those terms, that idea makes sense too: Take a lump of clay that is shaped into a pot to hold dates. Then, when no longer needed, it is pulled apart and re-worked into a grain storage unit. As such, the object is reborn.

The structure of the book wants to mirror the duality that pervaded every aspect of ancient Egypt: life and death, day and night, etc. Two opposites that complemented each other, and which were natural halves of one same cycle. A duality that is perfectly applicable to organic creations.

In the first half, BIRTH, we will deal with how these items came to be. We will start by looking at the earth as a prime natural material, and then go through the multiple ways in which plants have played – and continue to play – a fundamental role in our lives on Earth. This will naturally lead us to think of the animals that feed from those plants, and whose products are also essential for human survival. As part of that, we will see how our own bodies play a part in how we relate, and react, to nature. In this process, we will answer questions about the properties of natural materials, the objects that were made with them and the ways in which they became a fundamental part of different cultures. We will also immerse ourselves in the uses of organic compounds for other purposes, such as medical remedies and recipes.

Each of the three chapters (earth, plants and animals) will try to inspire you to realise the value of organic objects and incorporate them into your routines and ultimately a new way of life.

In the second half, REBIRTH, we will look at what happens to objects when their main life period is over. Through some ethnographic examples, we will discover that some of the modern principles of sustainability, such as repairing and repurposing, have a long history in traditional societies. We will be able to answer questions such as: How can we make use of ancient traditions and knowledge to tackle sustainable issues nowadays? How can we combine them with the latest technology to build a healthier and safer world?

All this knowledge will give us inspiration to take on a more sustainable approach to our lives, through reducing, reusing, recycling, repairing and rethinking what we use and how we use it. We will focus on the main polluting industries in the modern world: the food production and consumption, the building and the clothing sectors, as well as analysing waste creation and management.

Throughout both parts I (Birth) and II (Rebirth), we will trace the presence and use of organic materials in various modern cultures to help us complete and confirm what the ancient Egyptian objects, amongst others, seem to be telling us about their purpose and life. This approach will also help give us a global, decentralised perspective about the topic and the current situation.

If our connection with nature is such an inherent part of us as humans, what is hindering it now?

By the time you finish reading this book, I hope you will have a different outlook on organic objects throughout time, and that you become inspired to see the ways in which the ancestral knowledge linked to them can be used, adapted and enhanced through the use of modern technology to achieve a more sustainable society.

Part I: Birth

Before we start talking about organic objects in ancient Egypt and beyond and their importance for our modern lives, it is essential to clarify what we mean by 'organic'. This is particularly relevant since, in recent times, the word organic has become widely used in relation to food. Organic food can be defined as that 'grown without the use of synthetic chemicals, such as human-made pesticides and fertilizers, and which does not contain genetically modified organisms (GMOs)', whether of plant or animal origin. Essentially, it is food that has been produced in a natural way, the way it was traditionally done before humans started developing ways to extend crop life and create more attractive vegetables. Thanks to pesticides and fertilisers, it became possible, for example, to create large-scale agricultural exploitation and eat strawberries all year round. However, in recent years, the climate crisis, paired with a better awareness of the damaging effects of these artificial enhancers, has led to their social rejection and to an increase in the commercialisation of 'organic' food products.

Although organic food refers to a natural way of production, the truth is that 'organic' makes direct reference to the internal composition of products rather than to their production process; it is also independent of their use as food, clothing or even decoration. Put simply, organic objects can be defined as 'relating to chemical compounds that contain carbon and mainly or ultimately come from living things.' Basically, most natural things that surround us are organic, with the exception of minerals and metals. The ground that we stand on, the plants that grow from it and the animals that feed on those plants, all are organic, as are their by-products. And since we are animals ourselves, our by-products, such as a mother's breast milk, are also organic.

Earth, plants and animals exist in nature independent of the use that humans choose to give to them. In certain cases, they can be used without any processing; in others, they require some modification. Either way, an organic product is born out of them, and this is what part I of this book talks about. How do we go about structuring this? As we have already remarked, the vast majority of what surrounds us in the natural world is organic, so we could have as many categories as objects made of organic materials. Classifying them according to their function in society is also complicated, since, as will be seen through the book, organic products are closely interrelated, and their use overlaps across many spheres of human life. In the end, nature's own division seems the most appropriate: there are those products which come from the soil itself, those which come from plants (which includes trees, fibres and cereals) and those which come from animals (including humans). Once we have established those three simple groups, we can think of what is common to all of them in terms of their symbolical and practical properties as materials. Thus, in the introduction to each chapter, we will discuss the significance that soil, plants and animals have for various cultural groups, even before they are turned into objects. This is especially significant for the first chapter, Born from Earth, as earth is home for the other two, plants and animals. Across the three chapters, we will be asking ourselves questions such as: What are the symbolical meanings of soil beyond providing a living ground for a variety of living beings? What role do plants and animals play in keeping us connected to nature and how can we use their by-products to live a more sustainable life?

Because these are universal elements shared across many cultures, we can draw on the information from different human groups, present and past, to understand them in all their nuances. In terms of the past, this book has a strong focus on ancient Egypt. But let us focus for a moment on how we can still have enough information about organic materials from over 3,000 years ago. In Egypt, we are very lucky that dry and hot weather conditions have allowed for so much food to be preserved. But another key reason for their preservation is the fact that food offerings were included in tombs. Even though this would seem a waste of food to us, it had a strong symbolical and practical function for the ancient Egyptians.

Living for eternity

If you were given the choice to take something into the afterlife, what would it be? The ancient Egyptians had their priorities: yes, there were plenty of objects they needed to navigate the afterlife, but first and foremost, they needed food. For that reason, their relatives made sure to leave food offerings in the tomb, such as bread and beer. That is the reason why we can stand in front of a loaf of bread that is over 3,000 years old in a museum such as the Museo Egizio de Torino. It is rare to find processed food in the archaeological record if it has not been given a ritualistic role, unless a sudden event takes place, such as the eruption of Mount

Vesuvius in Pompeii; food is something people do not tend to leave behind. However, thanks to the Egyptian concept of the afterlife, those edible objects, and also things like furniture, jewellery, clothes and even toys, have been preserved. But the ancient Egyptians, ever the practical civilization, did not only take these objects, but they also came up with a way of having everything they needed at hand.

They achieved this through a combination of practicality and magic. Food, clothes and utensils were no doubt needed to continue living life just as before passing away. And just as we often take travel-size versions of what we consider to be our everyday essentials, the ancient Egyptians (or rather, those who could afford to do so) made sure to put in their tombs plenty of miniature versions of their most precious belongings. The inconvenience of having to carry all these goods was easily resolved, as for example, amulets of objects could, through the power of magic, become life-size equivalents if required. This process of the small becoming large was not always necessary, which is obvious from the amount of large furniture we find in tombs such as that of Kha, or the better-known tomb of Tutankhamen. Beds, cabinets, tables, etc. bear witness to the upper class's determination to bring all their riches with them. But many other everyday life objects, such as sieves to make bread and containers for ointments, were symbolically added to the tomb so that they could be of use at any time. They differ in size, from tiny dinnerware befitting of a doll house to larger house models, but a large majority of them have in common that they reproduce the material they were made of in real life. Sometimes, they even improve that material, with some sycamore boxes that imitate the nooks and knots of more expensive wood.

In addition, ancient Egyptians loved metaphors, so anything that evoked the journey that the deceased made into the afterlife, from day to night, from light to darkness, was also bound to feature in the tomb.

Although, as I explained in the introduction, these tombs represent a very small percentage of the population, their metaphorical references to universal things such as preparing food and drink, mean that they can help complete our understanding of everyday life. On the other hand, house remains, the vast majority of them made of earth, offer a much wider picture of social strata and allow us to have a more realistic grasp of the different circumstances under which those universal themes could develop.

Chapter 1: Born from earth

Earth is such an obvious part of our lives that we often forget how essential it is for our existence. It not only serves as the ground we walk on, but also as the place where we grow our vegetables and that our animals feed on. For the best part of history, it has also been a dominant building material across the world. Even now, it is estimated that between 30% to 50% of the world's population (approximately 3 billion people!) live in buildings made of earth.

Earth also represents our homeplace and, throughout history, human groups have established a strong connection to the land they inhabit. Soil is the connecting point between the Earth and us, the sensorial evidence that we live on the outer crust of a rounded planet. Even before humans became sedentary, landscape features played an essential part in the way humans related to the environment. Rivers, trees and mounds marked the boundaries of a communal space or the furthest point to which a group would move when looking for food or working their tools. No doubt, though, all landscape features are rooted in, and survive through, the existence of soil itself. It is this nurturing nature that has made cultures across time and space refer to our planet as Mother Earth, and even in Western countries nowadays we continue to use this expression, especially when talking about the need to protect our home from the effects of climate change.

In this respect, both the concept of Earth and the physical soil are generally considered female. It will not come as a surprise then to hear that all the things that can be made from this soil, such as pots, are connected to the female sphere. For example, within the Luo people in East Africa, only women can carry out pottery making. Pots are seen in the same way as babies: only females have the power of bringing them into life. These links to fertility and womanhood are so strong that Luo women take to eating earth, as they believe in this way their blood is better and they have more chances of having children.

This association between soil and women, and their respective by-products, was not alien to ancient Egypt. Organic ingredients are a very important part of Papyrus Ebers, a medical papyrus which contains a wealth of recipes destined to cure all kinds of ailments. If one organic product is good, a combination of several, such as soil and female fluids, can only increase the chances of the treatment being successful. This is apparent in the number of remedies that combine pots or bricks with milk (whether human milk or cow milk, as both are seen as coming from mothers and are therefore equivalent concepts to the ancient Egyptians). For example, a remedy to improve sight involves warming chips of a pot in fresh milk, which is then to be drunk by the patient. In ancient Egypt, just as in many other cultures, eating and drinking was a way of obtaining the powerful and magical properties attributed to what was consumed.

In the case of the Luo people, women and children of both genders eat earth as a way of guaranteeing that they will perform well the role society expects from them, and also to make sure that they keep their place in the community. Even at present, in certain villages in Spain, the lime found in the local mountains is added to food such as bread, as the folklore of the area says that it provides energy. Eating soil to interiorise its properties is perhaps an extreme way of keeping in touch with your place of birth, but other ways of maintaining this contact are also possible. The Luo also rub native soil on the face of someone who is going away, to guarantee that they do not lose that connection with their community. A tradition which might seem a bit different to us is that of relatives taking bags of earth with them when they visit members that have left the community to move elsewhere.

In the Western world, the identification of our native land with the actual soil that we walk on, has been largely lost. It is true that speakers of some languages, such as Spanish, specifically refer to the land when expressing a longing for home (*echo de menos mi tierra* translates as 'I miss my land'). The English 'home turf' also builds on the idea of soil as an embodiment of the place, perhaps going further in evoking the exact qualities of the soil than a vaguer 'my land'. Even within the same language, there are a variety of ways to express this attachment; Irish people, for example, use the expression 'the auld sod' to refer to their homeland. However, this is as far as the connection between land and soil gets, and I doubt anyone in my close circle would bring bags of earth to relatives to remind them of their place of origin. Yet, despite this apparent disconnection, certain visual gestures that we might be used to regardless of our background, such as the Catholic Pope kissing the ground upon arrival to a place, are not only a sign of respect, but a reflection of this identification between soil and land.

We also find echoes of this ancestral association in a famous ancient Egyptian text, the *Tale of Sinuhe*. This incredible story has reached us in full thanks to the work of ancient scribes that copied it time and again, and its broader themes and perspective are so current, no one would guess it is around 4,000 years old. The *Tale of Sinuhe* tells the story of a palace worker who flees the country following the pharaoh's assassination; after spending much time away, he asks the current pharaoh to allow him to return home to die. In fact, it is Sinuhe that tells us his own story after death, as a way of highlighting the importance of dying in the homeland, as well as of fulfilling the complex set of rites needed to go onto the afterlife in ancient Egypt. Sinuhe's reaction when he hears that the ruler has accepted his request leaves no doubt about the strong link between the idea and the physical reality of the land:

It [the royal letter] was read to me and I prostrated myself / I touched the earth/ and scattered it on my hair.

The following lines go on to highlight the joy caused by this regal permission. Not only does Sinuhe want to touch the ground when he hears the news; he also takes this connection further by throwing the earth over his head. Even though that soil belongs to a foreign land and not to his home, it is the vehicle that expresses his identification with his homeland and his happiness at the very thought of being there again.

Even Sinuhe's own name evokes the importance of organicity. In the following chapter, which focuses on plants, we will get to know more about the symbolism of different trees for the ancient Egyptians; for now, it is worth remarking that his name translates as 'the son of the sycamore'.

The idea that human beings are drawn to the land we were born in is not surprising, as many cultures believe that we come from earth. Even the Bible says, in the book of Genesis, that God modelled 'man' from clay. Another example is that of an apocryphal gospel story (which is also featured in the Quran) in which baby Jesus models birds with clay, and them blows on them/commands them to fly. It seems that, throughout their lives, people do not lose this attachment, just as Sinuhe continues yearning for his home. If you have ever attended a Christian funerary service, you might have heard the expression 'ashes to ashes, dust to dust', which also reflects a return to the place where we first came from, materialised in burying the dead underground. But, for many cultures, including the ancient Egyptian, death is not the end of the story. Yes, the soil they are buried in is organic, but they also need to be offered food to be kept alive.

In some cultures, this attachment is so strong, that the dead must be buried within the house to represent this return. The house is a life-giving place, whether before or after death. For that very reason, clay from walls is scraped off for various purposes across cultures. In the case of the Luo, it is another source of iron when they do not collect earth to eat from the fields; 'clay from the wall' was also familiar to the ancient Egyptians, and it is listed as a component in a remedy for a poultice or dressing used to fight skin problems.

I am sure by now you have come to realise that, because of the symbolic power soil has, it is a central part in the lives of many different cultures. But, as is often the case, that symbolism comes from its practicality in improving living conditions: it is the perfect material to build earthen houses which keep cool in the summer and warm in the winter, or to build pots that preserve food between harvests.

Living in a material world

I have a vivid image of the first time I entered an Egyptian mudbrick house. It was virtually the only mudbrick house left in that village of the Egyptian northwest Delta, the rest having been replaced by the usual unfinished concrete and red brick blocks of flats that have now peppered Egypt's urban landscape for decades. There it stood, made proud by age, sandwiched between concrete slices. So many original features were preserved, that it was both a blessing and a curse: I knew immediately I was unlikely to find another mudbrick house as steeped in the past as that one. Its entrance was pretty much a continuation of the earthen floor, which had been moulded into a raised semicircle in front of the door in order to protect it from water. Also, with water in mind, the roof was topped by a heavy pile of hay which gave it a cartoon-like look. The house was not permanently inhabited anymore, but the family's grandmother still called it home. Her face lit up with a toothless smile as she paraded me around, beaming with pride at the now almost empty house where she had been brought up. As is often the case with mudbrick houses in large parts of Egypt, the house was now mainly used to keep animals, so children had been replaced by geese which were being fed in the back of the house. Although the family had built a 'proper', 'modern' house opposite (all adjectives used by the owners), the grandmother still had her room upstairs and she very much preferred spending time there.

As she walked up to her bedroom, her feet matched the shape of the mud treads, with their middle section being eroded by the constant going up and down. On the side of the staircase, a niche had been carved into the mud wall and that now empty space, I was informed, used to hold an oil lamp to help climb the stairs when there was no daylight. What was most striking when you got to the top of the stairs is that you had to be careful not to fall back to the ground floor through the patio that had been unintentionally formed by the collapse of approximately half of the upper floor. The geese had taken over that now sunny and well-ventilated space. On the side of the floor, which was still standing, stood a range of mud bins in different shapes and sizes, some with grain inside. One flowed into the next and into the next forming a single entity, and the tallest one in the corner continued into the beam that supported the plastic sheets and hay which formed the roof cover.

The plasticity of every detail was striking, and my informant was keen on emphasising the advantage of living in such a house, which was almost a living thing in itself. It served to keep cool in the summer and warm in the winter, all famous qualities of earthen buildings. Contrasting with the point of view of the elderly, younger informants saw modern houses as being more comfortable and cleaner, thus having an advantage over their old equivalents. One reason for this was that in practice, the loss of knowledge, the adaptation to constraints of different kinds and the lack of maintenance prevented the buildings from fulfilling many of the original functions they were designed for, such as temperature control. But there was – and there is – a more important factor, and that is social pressure. It is important because it weighs heavily on Egyptian perception of mudbrick houses; imported materials are considered a mark of progress, and their use has contributed heavily to the disappearance of mudbrick-making skills and traditions.

These processes of change are, of course, essential to bear in mind when we consider ancient Egyptian houses. No matter how hard to trace, they play an immense part in the decisions that lead to the disappearance of cultural tradition, in any form and shape. We will deal more in detail with those processes in modern times and how they have affected traditional architecture in recent decades in part II of this book. From a global perspective, they tie in with some of the other events which were mentioned in the foreword: the invasion of plastic and the rise of a disposable culture.

Before those changes came into place, for millennia, earthen houses were deemed the natural building solution in many regions of the world. Not only were locally available materials well-adapted to the environment – when used properly – in terms of temperature, for example, but they were also financially and ecologically sustainable in that they did not require unnecessary transport. What they did require was regular maintenance, and in most cases, this would have turned into a family and communal event, just as it is nowadays in present Mali. Once a year, just before the start of the rainy season, the entire village of Djenné comes together to help plaster their famous mosque, the largest mudbrick building in the world, and preserve it from wear and tear. This need for maintenance stems from the organic character of the materials; not only are mudbrick houses built with earth, but their walls are also plastered with it. In addition to the straw mixed in the mud, many other organic elements, such as wool, can be added to the mixture, with a compacting role in mind.

Mud plaster does not only have a practical function, serving to protect façades from weathering and from animal and human actions, but it also serves as a base for paint, turning walls into canvases. Paint is both a way to further protect the façade, and a means of expressing cultural identity in ways that exceed architectural choices. It is a way of manifesting your individuality, as well as a vehicle to express your place in the rest of the community. For example, drawings of ships or planes are a common feature of mud houses in Muslim countries to indicate that that person has already undertaken the obligatory lifetime trip to Mecca. These paintings display piety and duty fulfilment, as well as pride before other neighbours. Through them, everyone can rejoice at an event that is meaningful for the entire community. What is even more incredible is that a similar tradition already existed in ancient Egypt. During their lives, well-to-do individuals would travel to Abydos, where they believed the god Osiris rested, and then portrayed this pilgrimage on their own tomb walls. Although, nowadays, the paint is mostly synthetic, plant-based dyes and paints have been used for millennia, as will be mentioned later on.

But it could be said that the biggest advantage of mud as a building material is its flexibility. If there is a sudden need to separate a space, for example, a mud wall can easily be raised. Mud can also be taken off from, or added to, previously existing structures. It can be removed from walls to create niches, as described above, which can replace cupboards. Storage spaces can also be created by adding mud; if there is a need for containers, these can be shaped against a house main wall, which can act as the back wall. In traditional Egyptian houses, mud can also be packed along the façade of the house to build what are called *mastabas*, or mud benches. These benches have an important social function, connecting the family to the rest of the community. Families often sit out there with kids playing around; historically, if other members of the community came back at the end of the day from working in the fields, a drink could be offered to them there and a chat was encouraged, without the need to intrude into the more private space inside the house.

And speaking of drinking and eating, we cannot forget about an essential element of family and community life, the oven. The oven sits in the courtyard of the house or often in open spaces between houses, to be shared by several households; the archaeological record tells us that this was also often the case in ancient Egyptian towns. The reasons for this are obvious; getting rid of the fumes is easier this way, but it also works efficiently in providing a space for different families to fulfil the need to make bread, a fundamental staple food across history. This role, together with the fact that the oven itself is made of mud, means it completely embodies the concept of organic. Needless to say, the oven can also provide a source of warmth for those around.

The advantages of using mud for house building, but also for furniture and 'appliances' are, thus, endless, and all these creations intertwine and complement each other in a way that is befitting of their natural origins.

In part II of this book, we will delve into how current builders (architectural practices in the vast majority of cases) can use natural materials in an effort to develop more efficient and cleaner buildings and take advantage of nature to create incredible houses which fit well within their surroundings. The colours and textures of the materials can be carefully chosen to avoid the destruction of ecosystems and landscapes that so often comes with property development. In conjunction with specialised craftsmen and drawing on information accumulated through millennia, architects can achieve the right proportions and ingredients in order to make the most of earth's temperature-regulating properties, creating energy-efficient houses and reducing carbon dioxide emissions. There is no end to how local and traditional knowledge and new production techniques can be combined to produce sustainable architecture, provided, of course, that this ancestral information is respected and recovered and does not get lost.

An incredible example of the combined application of cutting-edge technology to traditional architectural methods is a recent project which has used 3D printing to build a mud house. The possibilities are endless: with a cheap material, houses could be built in a matter of a couple of months and be fully adapted to their natural environments, avoiding the costs and the pollution that come with the transportation of materials.

If we follow this path, the future of architecture will definitely face the challenges of climate change naturally and successfully: using nature respectfully, nature will be saved.

The inspiration for earthen architecture is slowly vanishing, and we must use our best efforts to save it and record it. Sadly, cities like Sana'a in Yemen, which features some of the tallest mudbrick buildings in the world, are no-go areas for tourists at the moment due to the devastating ongoing war which has caused a humanitarian crisis of terrible, long-lasting consequences, as well as destroying the millenary heritage of the Yemeni people.

Sana'a was classed as a World Heritage Site by UNESCO in 1986 and no doubt, when it is again possible, the country will benefit from the return of tourists to this unique beacon of mudbrick architecture. Djenné, in Mali, another World Heritage Site since 1988 featuring, as was previously mentioned, the largest mud mosque in the world, has also been threatened by the combat between Daesh and the main Al-Qaeda branch in the Sahel.

Another amazingly preserved place is Tiébelé, in Burkina Faso. It is an isolated site only visitable by a lucky few, but it is that protection that has maintained the architecture and kept the village life intact for centuries. As well as being made of mud, these houses are beautifully hand-painted with geometrical patterns. Even the paint itself is made of clay.

These communities are the depositaries of a world heritage that has been preserved for millennia and it is our global responsibility to help them maintain their traditional earthen structures and the ways of living and cultural knowledge associated to them.

Beyond this Earth

Earth is, as we have seen, fundamental to the living. However, as explained in the introduction to this chapter, for many cultures the role of earth exceeds this life. The tomb itself is already an earthen home for the person who has died, one that sometimes overlaps with the functioning family home, as burials are placed there. But for the ancient Egyptians it was not only a place for the deceased; their physical rebirth also took place in this earthen space. We already remarked in the introduction that, across many cultures, there is an intimate relationship between life, women and earth, and this trio features again in ancient Egyptian tombs.

According to research by scholars such as Kara Cooney, for women to be reborn they needed to temporarily turn into men, so they could produce the foetus that the Egyptians believed men passed onto women through intercourse. This, she explains, would account for the fact that the female figures portrayed in coffins wore the red colours usually associated with men and were referred to in the spells that decorated them with male pronouns. Before this new interpretation, these anomalies had been interpreted as grammatical mistakes or modifications made to coffins when a female relative died before the male the coffin was intended for. Again, the connection between earth and the female world, and the power of organic elements is highlighted by these beliefs.

There is a period of ancient Egyptian history, called the Middle Kingdom (ca 2030–1650 BCE), during which we find an even more obvious association between houses and tombs, in the form of clay models placed near burial surfaces. The significance of these models has long been the object of discussion by archaeologists. Given the place where they were found, it has often been suggested that they would have been signalling the location of a tomb; however, beyond that, discussion has focused mainly on whether they are representative of real houses, or they merely use some schematic domestic features to decorate offering trays. It is true that many of them show signs of having been exposed to fire, suggesting a ritual function. They are usually rather simple objects that often just hint at house features, such as patios, rather than developing them fully. Still, there are other models that are far more detailed. Traditionally, they were dismissed as reliable representations of houses because they looked far from sophisticated and their proportions were rather careless, even though some of them even feature porticos and staircases linking floors. Based on a comparison with existing Egyptian mudbrick houses, I believe that many of them do represent real houses, or rather, sections of those houses. Their features are key schematic clues that give us a perfectly plausible idea of something that can be built with mud – but we only come to realise these things when actually looking at traditional Egyptian houses and, for example, how common it is to have this sort of roof terrace accessed by a staircase (as was the case for the house I described earlier).

In fairness, house models are not an uncommon feature since the Neolithic period. This period, which starts at different times depending on world regions, is defined as one where plants and animals were domesticated, agriculture was developed, and permanent settlements were formed. We then find clay models of houses all the way from the Near East to Southeast Europe, made of the much-favoured mud, mirroring the materials that were being used for real buildings. These buildings would have had mud floors, bed platforms, benches, storage units and more, just as our Egyptian house earlier on. Building with mud was so popular then, that Mirjana Stevanovic has even suggested calling this period 'the age of clay'. The emphasis given to houses is not strange if we bear in mind, like Dušan Borić says, that physical buildings had just become a central social institution and symbol. The household would then remain a fundamental unit of society for millennia.

Nevertheless, house models do not always reflect real building materials; there are models of houses made inside ancient Egyptian tombs which are made of wood. They appear to represent ideal compounds for the nobility, almost like mansions that could feature in magazines nowadays. They feature lakes and trees almost overshadowing architectural features; others reproduce workshops, stables, bakeries and breweries in all sorts of details, including tools, animal parts, containers and clothing.

Life-giving vessels

Earth offers immense creative and sustainable possibilities. Whether it is in raw form, like mud, or baked, like clay, virtually anything can be made out of it with the right tools and in the correct proportions.

While earthen architecture is not suitable or traditional for every part of the world, containers made of earth, whether raw or fired, have been an ever-present feature of human societies for millennia. The need for them is obvious; everyone that lives a sedentary life wants to store food and liquid. But even in the cases where storage is performed differently – for example, the Eskimo keep their food in carved ice compartments under their igloos – clay pots are still used for cooking. Earth provides a convenient, reusable, and readily available material. If you observe your surroundings, you will realise how much it still features around you. Plant pots are a prime example of the kind of earthen container anyone might have in their house. Earth capacity to withstand heat and to maintain the temperature of its contents also make it ideal for food preparation and preservation. In fact, you may have some clay dishes at home which are suitable for the oven. Conversely, if you have ever visited or are from a Mediterranean country, you might have used what in Spain is called a *botijo*, an earthenware pitcher that keeps water as cool as if it were in the fridge. It is that universal usefulness that justifies clay's wide use and that puts it ahead of the game compared to modern materials, such as plastic. In turn, it is also what explains its archaeological relevance. Pottery is essential for archaeologists; it allows us to date objects that we find in the same context as these pots, and it even opens a window into the relationships between cultures, whether neighbouring or distant ones. Its shape and size have been designed across human groups to fit their contents and their function. Just think of a water jug you might have at home, whose spout makes it easier to pour the liquid into a glass, and how it differs from a deep dish or a jam jar. Ancient Egyptian pots include all kinds of practical features; for example, a strainer jar from ca 3200 BCE, which can be found in the Brooklyn Museum, has a perforated top which allows for the pot contents to be filtered.

These shapes and sizes, combined with the remains within, allow us to know more about people's diets, community organisation and trade. The large amount of remains of both solids and liquids (cereals, wine, beer, fruits, etc.) give us an insight into what was available to whom, and we can compare this information with that extracted from skeletons to gain a better understanding about people's diets and their health implications. Community organisation can be inferred from pots and their contents, for example, in terms of crop redistribution from a temple/palace, or household production. Lastly, the types of pots and their contents can help us know what peoples were trading with others, what were their main products and how far they made it.

There is another thing that determines the shape of pots and that is the manner in which they wish to be stored or carried. For example, amphorae that have a large and pointy bottom – apparently hard to stand up – fit very conveniently in between the wooden boards of a ship's hold. Other irregularly bottomed pots could be secured by partially burying them underground, which further helped preserve the temperature of the contents. For carrying, as well as the obvious handles, pot surface marks show that other organic materials such as woven nets, which are also organic objects, were used to help transport large pots in ancient Egypt. As has already been mentioned, organic materials intertwine and complement each other in many ways, not only practically, but also conceptually; for example, Nubian clay bowls (present day south of Egypt/north of Sudan) from ca 3200 BCE, have painted designs that imitate basketry. Interestingly, the walls of these conical bowls are extremely thin (so much so, that they are called 'eggshell ware', evoking yet another organic source).

But pots were not always made in the size that fitted their real purpose in ancient Egypt; as has already been explained, miniatures in tombs provided convenient versions of real pots to take into the afterlife. This includes full sets of cooking implements, such as the one dated from 1650–1550 BCE which can be found at the World Museum in Liverpool.

So, as we have seen, pottery has so many uses that it is no wonder that we can see it being used everywhere across history. In certain instances, pots can be even used as a building feature.

In Naqada, a famous Upper Egyptian village where pot making is a long-standing tradition, it is common to see them aligned in boundary walls or embedded in mud and stacked in large quantities to form building walls.

The fact that pottery is made from earth is not only the source of its useful properties, it is also the reason behind its hugely symbolic significance. Throughout this chapter, we have mentioned the link between earth and creation, channelled through women. We have also talked about the perceived healthy properties of eating mud. Both these links feature again when it comes to clay pots. The special characteristics of their earthen material, together with the power they obtain from the liquids or foods they contain, make them an essential component of many medicinal remedies, which in Egypt are often grounded in magic. Their function, both practical and symbolical, can also dictate the decoration applied to them. For example, some ancient Egyptian pots that feature clay protuberances in the shape of breasts, are believed to have contained milk to nurture the deceased. We will talk more about them in the Born from Animals chapter.

While I doubt any Western doctor would recommend eating clay as a cure to any ailment, mud does feature in many face masks, as it is commonly perceived to help purify the skin. Mud even has a recreational dimension, and you might have heard of 'mud runs', where participants get covered in mud as they overcome obstacles to complete a race.

In reality, the therapeutical associations of clay modelling are not entirely alien to us and have increasingly become more popular in the West. Nowadays, there are plenty of groups on social media platforms where you can learn more about clay modelling and pottery making. Modelling your own pottery cannot only help you create containers for cooking and storage that can replace plastic, like we will talk about in part II of the book, it can also be beneficial in a sensorial way. Many people take up pottery making as a hobby and as a way of establishing a connection with their surroundings. It is supposed to help concentration and to connect mind and body, and psychologists have proven that, just as other forms of craft, it reduces cortisol levels, the substance responsible for stress. You might think of this as a personal activity and something you would like to do on your own, but people also use Internet groups and websites like the Ceramic Arts Network, along with dedicated magazines, to get feedback and learn and share tips with other people that have the same interest. There is even a kind of 'YouTube for clay enthusiasts' called Claystation, where you can access online courses, visit channels, create playlists, socialise and attend live streaming.

In fact, the pottery making activities have become some popular that it is possible to book this experience as a team building activity for companies.

If a whole piece has a lot of symbolism, some cultures believe its broken parts maintain the powerful qualities of the object they came from and can interact in equal manner with the liquid they would have previously contained. We have already mentioned the remedy to improve sight cited in Papyrus Ebers, a lotion which is prepared by warming up chips of a new *hennu* pot in fresh milk. Sometimes, in ancient Egypt, we have names of pots whose shape or function we do not know, but we do know they are pots thanks to the determinative that appears at the end of the word. A determinative is a hieroglyph that explains what kind of object or living creature we are talking about, be it a pot, a bird or a person (qualifying even gender and age). In this case, the chips of that pot, combined with a vivifying liquid such as milk, have the power to improve visual problems.

Although pots were used so frequently in the past that it is not unlikely they broke accidentally, we cannot rule out them being broken on purpose. If we look at the plant pots around us today, some have been pierced at the bottom to allow the water to drain out. But, even when they were made on purpose, it did not necessarily have to be with practical purposes. As Julia Budka explains, it is a common feature of many cultures across time and space to break pots in association to a moment of collective gathering, which can be conveying excitement, anger or grief. Many people are familiar with the Greek tradition of breaking plates at weddings, which is often depicted in Hollywood movies.

In ancient Egypt, we also encounter different instances of pots being broken, which can be linked to rituals. The most famous of them is referred to in texts as "the breaking of the red pots". These pots, as well as being broken, had been given 'killing holes' to render them useless. The texts link the breaking of these pots to execration writings, as well as the funerary ceremony and food. Execration texts are those that contain names of enemies, including foreign foes, written on a medium which can then be destroyed, thus causing those people's symbolical destruction. The archaeological and written evidence for them is confusing though, and pot-breaking findings could also be related to the cult of the ancestors rather than focusing on avoiding evil.

The fact that broken parts of pots have symbolical meanings, does not mean they did not also have pragmatic, day-to-day function, and this can be seen in what are commonly referred to as ostraca. Ostraca (ostracon in singular) is a Greek word used to describe the fragments of both limestone and pottery that were used in ancient times for the purposes of writing. The kind of writing we can find in them is casual and often consist in annotations, draft texts or the odd name of a person, so we can think of them as ancient post-it notes. Occasionally, we also see them being used to practice drawing, although this is more common in the case of the limestone flakes.

Conversely, the process of sticking broken pots back together has had not only a historical practical function, helping to extend the useful life of the container, but also symbolical meanings which continue nowadays; they can be seen, for example, in the Japanese tradition of marking repair lines with bright colours. But we will look at that in detail in part II of the book, when we talk about recycling and repairing.

Clay pots are useful for cooking, storage, decoration, and modelling clay can help you relax and focus. Pottery's practical and symbolical undertones are so varied and so embedded in culture, that it is unlikely that any artificial material, such as plastic, could ever replace it.

Crafty solutions

In the previous section, we have sung the praises of pottery as an essential by-product of earth, both practically and symbolically. Traditionally, these skills were passed on from generation to generation, and many craftsmen have learnt the trade from their parents and grandparents and know how to best make the paste for the different pots, the tricks to prevent them from cracking and the techniques to make them more water-tight. There is a further dimension to that connection with the past. Some pottery makers help archaeologists recreate ancient pots and tools and create educational material that can then be used in activities at museums and learning centres; they make replicas which help preserve the original objects. Sometimes, museum visitors are allowed to touch and even manipulate the items they are looking at and, in doing so, they greatly contribute to making culture more accessible.

However, pots are by no means the only useful object to be made of soil. For starters, there are other clay objects that can help create and preserve food. Bread moulds were also made from clay, and just as a cake tin does for us today, they helped give shape to this essential element of Egyptian cuisine. We have seen that pots made, and continue to make, great containers for food; to help with content preservation, they could also be sealed by unfired pieces of mud used as plugs.

The truth is that soil has contributed greatly to all the areas of life that we talk about throughout this book. Not only has it been essential throughout history to make buildings, it has also provided practical implements such as clay oil lamps, hundreds of different mud storage containers and pigeon holes, a home version of the full-size mud pigeon houses to breed these useful birds. Some further mud elements cover needs which we might not be familiar with, but that are essential for certain communities. For example, in Qurna, in the south of Egypt, a traditional structure was a large circular, open-topped mud tower which served as a bed, and children were placed there to keep them safe from scorpions, though there were also large, rectangular mud beds for adults.

In chapter 2, we will have the chance to see the process through which plants ended up turning into clothes. But, as we will see throughout the book, one of the strengths of organic objects is how easily and effectively they combine with others to achieve a purpose. So, just because clothes are made of plants, it does not mean that soil stops playing a part: a fundamental development in the weaving process, loom weights, were made of baked clay.

The contribution of clay to personal ornaments did not stop there: from single beads to pendants or earrings, soil always helped to keep the link between the practical and the symbolical worlds.

Needless to say, there are few clearer tools to combine these two worlds than the act of writing, and soil was pioneer in this development through the appearance of clay tablets. The earliest examples preserved come from southern Iraq and date to around 3200 BCE. Although first used for accountancy rather than literary purposes, they were the first portable writing support, as well as being reusable. By smudging the cuneiform characters carved in them, they could be inscribed again with new symbols. The only inconvenience was that they were rather small and heavy, but, not surprisingly, two other organic-based materials would later come to perform the tablets' role in a more efficient way: papyri, made of plants, and parchment, made of animal skin.

Chapter 2: Born from plants

After our previous chapter, we have come to realise the extent to which earth plays a part in our lives. It provides the ground we stand on, as well as a building material. Interacting with it can help us keep our connection to the homeland and modelling it can make us relax and focus. But earth is also the breeding ground of plants, from which humans have historically obtained enough material to cover their shelter, food and creative needs.

The reason why plants provide such a big array of foodstuff and implements is that their various products can also generate a range of by-products that are relevant for all spheres of life. Fibres, trees and cereals, all of these can be considered plants. One of the main materials used across history, together with soil, is wood, which obviously comes from trees. So, it is no wonder that we have such a special relationship with plants. It feels so natural to be surrounded by them that we keep them in our home, not just because of the way in which they can help us regulate oxygen levels, but also because they are decorative and because of the personal connection we establish with them. You have probably heard that some people talk to plants, or you might talk to them yourself!

Plants have actually helped us live and stay alive from the very beginning of our history. Our ancestors would have used temporary structures made of reeds and branches to protect themselves from bad weather and they were able to move some distance in order to hunt and gather fruits to eat, which of course, fell from, or hung off, plants. Just as mud did, trunks and branches also played a fundamental part in early architecture. Trunks were worked into timber posts that could be used at regular intervals and crossed by other beams to provide strength.

Later on, with the development of agriculture, crops would become an essential part of human diet, one that has lasted until the present. Cereals, such as wheat and rice, are a staple food in most cultures across the world. In fact, some cultures follow a mostly plant-based diet, whether because of tradition, historical availability and events, or because their religious beliefs discourage eating meat. For example, it has been published that the Okinawa people in Japan follow a 96% plant-based diet. Incidentally, they have one of the longest life expectancies in the world. In Western countries, health and environmental considerations have prompted many people to only eat plant-derived food. Many believe that the current animal breeding industry is not sustainable, and that if we keep consuming cow meat at the rate that we are, the environment will be seriously damaged. There are others whose health is badly affected by meat consumption, or that choose a plant-based diet because they think meat production processes are cruel and unnecessary. There is also the issue that meat production uses up vast amounts of land, and in a world where large areas concentrate really high percentages of the global population, this is becoming more and more unsustainable. All these considerations tip the balance in favour of plant consumption for many people.

Interestingly, various places host world reserves or copies of seeds which could be artificially multiplied and grown to feed the world's population if need be. Although there are over 1,700 food crop gene banks across the world, the biggest one goes by the name 'Global seed vault' and is on a remote island in the Svalbard archipelago, halfway between mainland Norway and the North Pole. The whole idea, a secured repository surrounded by ice and built to withstand any catastrophe, seems out of a Bond movie. It has the capacity to store 4.5 million varieties of crops, and it aims to be a giant backup server of seeds from across the world. It is thought that keeping a variety of crops and increasing the different options will offer us a plan B, which given the evidence that suggests climate change will substantially affect agricultural produce in the future does not seem such a far-fetched idea.

If ice can provide a solution for the future preservation of crops, fire, most specifically its control, was instrumental to plants providing food for humans in the past. At least 790,000 years ago, our ancestors were increasing their options and improving their diet by using fire to eliminate the poison present in certain plants and extract their nutrients. Parts of plants also assisted in obtaining other more 'mobile' food. At least 500,000 years ago, humans started using wooden spears to hunt large animals. 'Digging sticks' would have also been used to extract insects from tree hollows, a behaviour which we can observe in chimpanzees and which early humans would have also exhibited. In addition, evidence from Poggetti Vecchi (in Tuscany, Italy) tells us that early Neanderthals, our closest ancient human relatives, already used fire to modify wood and make tools.

Other handy tools that our ancestors made were axe handles and boats. We actually evolved as a species thanks to wood, developing abilities such as sharpening sticks with teeth or stones, and the control of fire.

By around 26,000 years ago, humans also started creating more intricate tools with plants. A material already familiar to us, mud, helped preserve them through millennia and reach us. Stone Age clay imprints at the ancient Pavlov site in the Czech Republic are amongst the first evidence of basketry production. In fact, actual baskets have been found at Neolithic sites located in the Middle East and Kenya. There are also well-preserved examples in the west of the United States, dating to 10,000–11,000 years ago, and on the other side of the world, baskets made of bamboo were in use in China over 7,000 years ago. We have some incredibly well-preserved examples of basketry in ancient Egypt, which you can see in museums across the world. They look so new and current that you might actually own some older-looking ones. And it is not just their manufacture that would have been impressive, their size can also be remarkable. In the *Taking of Joppa*, a story featuring a man sent by the king to put an end to a servants' revolt, men are smuggled in human-size baskets, in a story that predates the famous Trojan horse by 500 years. While boasting battle tales are not always to be trusted, the truth is that the size of surviving examples suggest that such large baskets were materially and technologically possible.

Food for thought

We generally think about food and shelter as the two basic human needs. Shelter generally refers to buildings, though clothes also help protect us from the elements. We use plants to make both houses and garments, and, as has already been mentioned, they are a fundamental part of human diet across the world. But even though more and more people are adopting a vegetarian-heavy diet, the news is not all good. How has a natural dietary habit, which is so essential to our survival, and which has served us through millennia, come to destroy entire communities? How is it that by trying to be healthy we are behaving in a completely unsustainable way? Fads have a lot to do with it, as does globalization. An avocado toast might be an exotic and fashionable breakfast, and is indeed a healthier choice than a fry-up, but the huge demand for it in any season is having a really negative impact over the lives of certain human groups. The surge in avocado production areas to cover the global demand has led to violence and deforestation in places such as the state of Michoacán, in Mexico. Forests have been cleared with the aim of growing them and cartels have developed to control the production. They exert a violent law akin to that of drug ones, as groups take over local farmers' lands and even recruit temporary forced labourers. Still, boycotting these products is not a solution to the problem, as this would mean harming the livelihood of many humble families who depend on this trade.

It is not only the demand for fashionable fruits and vegetables that can have a negative effect over sustainability, but also the fact that people expect to have access to such food all year around. If you live in Europe, the days when you could only have strawberries in the summer are long gone; instead, now strawberries are grown in large greenhouses locally, as well as being imported from countries on the other side of the world. This incurs astronomical costs when it comes to transporting and packaging (which, more often than not, is done with plastic). Some time ago, a Reddit user posted a picture on the Internet which showed a plastic pot of pre-packed pear chunks with the following text stamped on its side: *Pears grown in Argentina. Packed in Thailand.* This product was being sold in a US supermarket and sums up the shocking and pointless structures surrounding food and vegetables trade. A similar case can be seen in much of the seafood sold in the US, which is labelled as being 'a produce of China', since it is cheaper to fillet it and package it there and send it back to the US than to carry out the process in Alaska, where the fish is originally caught.

This also has an effect on the country where the food is cultivated. For example, in Ethiopia, where *teff* is grown, a formerly commonly consumed grain has turned into a luxury, to the point that the government had to avoid exports of raw teff between 2006 and 2015 to avoid a food crisis.

In part II of the book, we will review the attempts being made globally to develop sustainable crops that can be both grown in their countries of origin and help feed other countries in need in a way that does not impact the planet negatively. We will also focus on the way that food waste can be repurposed to create by-products for consumption and beyond. Luckily, there are initiatives that attempt to foster collaboration to do this at corporate level, but we will also see how you can incorporate this into your everyday life with the resources available to you.

Dressing up the world around

Some of the memories of my earliest childhood with my grandmother are of making a type of lace which relies on bobbins.

Thread gets wrapped around each wooden piece and they are all hung off the top of a pillow-like implement, to which a cardboard pattern is fixed. In the intersection of each point of the pattern, a pin is placed to help guide the weaver, and the bobbins are skilfully moved to make the threads intertwine and follow the design down. Nowadays, it is by no means so commonplace, but there are still villages where women devote themselves to developing these patterns that can then be used to protect armrests, decorate garments or as table runners.

It does not get much more plant-based than using objects made of plants to turn other plants into garments, and wooden tools such as the ones I just described are present across different areas and cultures. What is incredibly striking is that the basic instruments of spinning and weaving have remained unchanged through millennia, making it easier for us to understand the techniques that were used in the past through modern comparison. We do not lack examples of early textiles; incredibly, in Catalhoyuk, in Turkey, there are remains from between 8,700 and 8,500 years ago, which would have been made with local oak fibres. The Tarkhan dress, found in the cemetery of the same name in Egypt and which has been most recently dated with radiocarbon to 3482–3102 BCE, is the oldest woven garment known to date which has been preserved almost in full. The incredible linen garment features a V-neck, with decorative folds on the chest and sleeves.

Prehistorian Ian Gilligan proposes a controversial theory: that clothing production was so important, that it was this, and not food, that prompted the development of organised agriculture. According to him, after the last ice age, global warming would

35

have prompted human groups in many areas to replace the animal hides used until then for textiles.

The use of textiles went beyond a means of dressing, it became a real way of distinguishing social classes. They also helped furnish and decorate houses, which were another sign of status.

Amongst one of the most important plants in antiquity was flax, which had multiple uses. Its seeds and oil are edible, and the latter could also be used as lighting fuel. In addition, flax fibres were used to create baskets and mats. But most importantly, linen, as it is best known, would become one of the main textile materials to be used until present, especially in warm countries, thanks to its breathable and cool qualities, and we have examples as old as 6900–6300 BCE. It was complemented by wool, which we will talk about in the Born from Animals chapter.

In the case of ancient Egypt, as Chiara Spinazzi-Lucchesi explains, the production of textiles was relevant to all spheres of life (and death), because they were gradually more and more used in Pharaonic times as shrouds for the deceased and as grave goods, which is the reason why so many of them have not only reached us but have done so in an excellent state of preservation. They also served as a means of payment, and this is another reason why they were produced in mass.

We have indeed a large amount of evidence of both textiles and their tools, like spindle whorls and shafts. We even find yarn wound into balls in many Egyptian sites, at a level that allows us to document all phases of textile production. Through them we can get to know details such as the fact that the yarn spun was not always immediately used for weaving, but sometimes kept for a later date. In Deir el-Medina, an ancient settlement we have already mentioned, spindle shafts were made of the best wood and whorls featured a softer kind. To help us reconstruct the world of textiles even further, ancient Egyptians portrayed weaving in wall reliefs, helping us confirm aspects of the fabric-producing sphere and its place in their society.

In fairness, some other tools made from plants that feature in the domestic sphere are less glamourous, like a broom made of reeds from 1539–1075 BCE currently stored in the Brooklyn Museum! This broom looks very much like one that could be found nowadays in rural settings across the world. In fact, the actual principle is no different from a broom you might have in your house, only this one does not require a plastic stick or artificial fibres, it is all completely natural.

Plants are actually everywhere when it comes to ancient Egyptian tomb reliefs. They decorate scenes, contributing to the sense of peace and harmony that the deceased would expect to have in the afterlife. In a hot, desertic country, there is nothing more desirable than a cool tree shade, next to a water source. For the Egyptians, the desert represented the enemies, while Egypt and the Nile were one and the same thing. Thus, the plants that could be found near the river were very important for them, so much so, that they even became the symbol of the north and south of the country. Upper Egypt, in the south, had the lotus as their symbol, while Lower Egypt, in the north, adopted the papyrus. This symbolism of plants extended much further, turning into a religious symbol. A common scene features the deceased smelling a fragrant lotus flower. That association between flowers and life here brings us memories of the links between clay and creation: the lotus was believed to be the first creature to have emerged out of chaos when the world was created and so was thought to have great powers associated with it, helping the deceased into the afterlife. We will explore that association further in the Flower Power section of the book.

Writing a page of history

In the Crafty Solutions section of chapter 1 we briefly touched on how clay was the first portable surface humans wrote on consistently. But it was a plant that enabled a great leap in terms of convenient writing sources and literary production: the papyrus. Although used to create a variety of objects, such as small boats, mats or sandals, it was its use as 'paper' that catapulted its fame until present times, where it is seen as a recognisable symbol of ancient Egypt by people of all ages across the world. Making it was no easy task, and it required skill as well as time. The process consisted of laying down strips together of the pith found inside the stalk and then applying pressure to dry the surface created by the addition of these strips. The stalks had to be previously preserved in water to keep their flexibility. We are lucky to have hundreds of documents that help us understand ancient Egyptian life and problems, such as letters, contracts, illustrated and legal documents, and religious texts. The first papyrus known comes from the tomb of the high official Hemaka (ca 2900 BCE), although nothing is written on it, while around 400 years later we have the first examples of administrative documents. Interestingly, papyri could be reused in different ways. Sometimes, the content was erased so that the papyrus could be written on again, as was done with clay tablets. Other times, it was covered in plaster, so that it could serve as a cartonnage, which is the name given to the cardboard-looking structures used to cover mummies. It is only one of many examples that show what great recyclers ancient Egyptians were.

But the role of plants in writing did not end at the paper; the tools used for writing on it were also made of plants. The scribes had kits of rush styluses that they wrote with. In the first century BCE, they would be replaced by reeds. To practice writing, they used wooden boards, and we have found several of these exercise boards, which artists also used to practice proportions and lines before drawing.

The biggest handicap with wooden objects is that, as other organic items, they are very vulnerable to rot. But we do know that, in the first millennia BCE, instruments made of reeds were used in sites such as Deir El Medina, in Egypt, so there is no reason to rule out that the first musical instruments in history could have been made of these perishable materials rather than more resilient bones.

Magically cured

Plants have been used as part of medicinal remedies since the beginning of times and are still a central part of medical traditions in countries such as China. People observed plants properties, sometimes accidentally, and used them to their advantage. Many plants are proven to have antiseptic, anti-inflammatory and sedative properties, amongst others. This knowledge would have been passed on from generation to generation, and it is so local that even nowadays many plants have many different names within the same country. Plants also form the basis of medicinal principles found in popular drugs such as Aspirin, whose main ingredient is acetylsalicylic acid, which is extracted from willows. Other plants have chemical properties which have been successfully tested in medical trials on issues such as tumoral suppression and cancer. Of course, the use of plants in medicine must be exercised with caution and the unsupervised ingestion of wild plants is generally discouraged. We must bear in mind that the conditions that plants have grown in throughout the millennia are not the same, neither is our metabolism. Certain plant extracts are still used in small quantities, for example as infusions, to help with digestion. You probably have had a peppermint or a camomile tea sometime after a heavy meal, and there is evidence that those plants have been considered helpful in that way for millennia. However, other plants are poisonous, or their usefulness strongly depends on the part of the plant being used, which means that ingesting one part instead of another can be fatal. Some plants that ancient sources guarantee to help with a certain ailment, are now known to have precisely the opposite effect.

As has already been mentioned, we have plenty of papyri from ancient Egypt which give us information about many aspects of life, and medicine is no exception. Papyrus Ebers contains abundant spells and remedies, in which plants feature prominently as part of recipes and concoctions. These remedies featuring plants could not only help cure headaches, diarrhoea or period pain, but could also assist in fixing baldness and sweaty feet, or in domestic tasks such as keeping mice away from the granary. Even if reproducing Egyptian remedies might not be the safest or wisest of things, seeing their vast knowledge of their environment and the degree to which they made use of natural resources, can inspire us to reflect more on the world around us and on the sustainable choices we can make for ourselves.

Ancient Egyptians suffered particularly from eye ailments, and physicians made sure to have plenty of tools at their disposal to treat diseases caused by insects at different times of the year. A very interesting wooden box, now in the Brooklyn Museum, has three powder compartments, to be used for each one of the three Egyptian seasons, winter, flood season, and summer. The hieroglyphs inscribed on it also express the usefulness of the powder to cure ophthalmia.

But there were plenty of other wooden objects involved in medicine and magic. In ancient Egypt, just as in many other ancient societies and some traditional societies nowadays, medicine and magic were deeply intertwined. For that reason, not only were the remedies accompanied by spells and rituals that guaranteed their correct functioning, but these helped protect, for example, children and pregnant women from the supernatural.

Often, these magical objects have been mistaken for toys. Although most modern toys are made of plastic, wood has always been a popular material for children's entertainment too. Both their material and their design influenced their interpretation. For example, 'paddle dolls' are ancient Egyptian flat wooden dolls which represent female bodies in a simple way. Many of them have beads attached to their heads, representing long hair, as well as dresses drawn on them. Although for a long time they were believed to belong to the children sphere, the newest interpretation is that they would have helped encouraged fertility and be related to rebirth into the afterlife.

The biggest challenge in archaeology is, of course, overcoming our bias and not assuming that objects are what we think they are just because we would give them that use nowadays, or because they remind us of other objects. So, in the same way as we assume a doll is a toy, we might not be prepared to interpret a rag ball as such. However, we find such an example in the Bristol Museum (UK). What looks like an old piece of material is indeed rolled into a ball, and judging from the fact that we have tomb representations which show children playing ball games, it was probably put there by the kid's parents so that they could play with it in the afterlife.

Giving examples of every single type of plant-based object that has reached us from the ancient world would take hundreds of books. But these brief examples help us get such a vivid account of human emotion and enable us to feel a connection with the people that used them like no other object can, regardless of time and geographical distance.

Flower power

Flowers are probably the most universally appreciated part of plants. These incredible organisms come in all imaginable sizes and colours. They can be as small as pins or as wide as a door. Flowers have a fundamental role in nature through enabling pollination, but humans have always particularly loved them for their beauty and fragrance. This is the case for most flowers, though there are also scary-looking ones, like snapdragon flowers, whose seed pods look like tiny human skulls when they dry. Given their appearance, it is no wonder that some historical cultures attributed supernatural properties to them. Part of the reason why flowers are so special is because they change at will; for example, some flowers only open at night, while some others can open as seldomly as once every forty years, attracting big crowds eager to witness such a unique event. It is as if they have a life of their own, because of course, they do, and react to stimuli in a way that could be seen as sharper than that of humans. They are affected by the sun, by darkness, by water or by the slightest hum of an insect in dramatic, life-changing ways.

Because of their smell, their look and even their touch, all cultures have always loaded flowers with meaning. Endless legends justify their names and appearance, and many of these tales feature tragic love stories which see both women and men being turned into flowers. In the famous Greek legend that gives origin to the word 'narcissistic', Narcissus, a self-centred young man who would make a good influencer nowadays, sees his vanity punished when he is turned into a daffodil after falling in love with his own reflection. Other legends link flowers to particular historical events. For example, a poem written by Canadian physician John McCrae during World War One, spoke of poppies growing fast amongst the graves of those that had died in the Belgian battlefields. As a result, the poppy became a symbol of those who had lost their lives in battle during both world wars. But red flowers are clearly evocative of blood in a broader context and, in Christian culture, for example, they have long been related to Christ and his death.

Generally, though, flowers tend to have positive connotations and have long been used to mark all sorts of celebrations. They are still often taken to hospitals across the globe when a person has had an operation or a baby is born, brides across the world carry bouquets for their wedding day and the tradition of laying flowers at tombs at least once a year is still important in many countries. Flowers are also really valued in some cultures for their protective properties; in Ireland, flowers are traditionally placed at the doorstep to ward off spirits and evil forces. The frequent close links between religious and popular belief are also obvious in the use of flowers. In the Christian religion, the Virgin Mary is celebrated with flowers in May, as in the northern hemisphere this is the peak of the spring season and the time when most flowers bloom. The way in which plants bridge the gap between religion and superstition also applies to other relevant figures, such as saints; for St Bridget's Day in Ireland (1 February) rushes are traditionally collected from wetlands and cut into 20–30 cm pieces in order to make crosses designed to ward off evil, fire and hunger. In fact, this festivity, of Celtic origins, was already really important in antiquity as a festival of fertility and as a mark of the beginning of spring. The abundance and relief the new season brought after a harsh winter was a significant reason for celebration.

Although flowers may seem immensely delicate, petals from thousands of years ago have survived until the present day. Incredibly, archaeological teams in Egypt have found flower garlands adorning mummies dated to the first millennia BCE. But if you are not terribly impressed by that, wait until you hear about a 30,000-year-old flower being brought back to life. It is a story that seems to have come out of the cartoon movie *Ice Age*. A squirrel stocks away a fruit in a burrow, just before the Ice Age kicks in. Then the burrow freezes, together with its contents. As a result, tens of thousands of years later, scientists manage to recover the fruit from its fossilised sediments and grow the flower from the fruit tissue. As much as there is something very charming about seeing a flower from a plant that lived at the same time as woolly mammoths, the reality that permafrost is thawing at a frightening rate can only help highlight the dramatic effects of climate change. According to scientist P. Buford Price, as permafrost melts further, we are likely to see more and more ancient seeds growing without human intervention, and this might not always be such a pleasant surprise.

Flowers appeared around 130,000 years ago, as we can tell from fossilised remains of plants. To date, they remain one of the most expressive ways of wishing other people well. There are infinite things you can use flowers for, from gifts, to decoration, and there are countless resources on the Internet which clarify the symbolism of colour, shape and place for different cultures. As you explore them, you will come to realise the many common trends in the ways humans across space and time have related to plants. But we get a heads-up of this special relationship in the next section.

Human roots

In the first chapter of this book, Born from Earth, we came to realise the strong symbolism that linked humans with earth right from the beginning of our history. And, since the vast majority of plants survive through being rooted in the soil, it only makes sense that there should be such a close connection too between plants and humans.

45

Right from the moment human groups tried to explain to themselves the origin of the world, they turned to nature for answers, and used any similarities they found to support the stories they came up with to understand their surroundings. For example, an ancient Mesopotamian myth asserted that the Earth was created using a reed mat. They also tried to explain how certain crafts, such as basketry, had come to be, and what their relationship to the origin of the world was. The Dogon of West Africa believe that their first ancestor put a square-bottomed basket he was given upside down and used it as a model to create a world with a square sky and a round Earth. It is no surprise that myths and ideas related to basketry appear all over the world, across the tens of thousands of years humans have been weaving them, since there are suitable plant twigs to make them across the globe. For the Guayaki Indians of eastern Paraguay, for example, this materialises in a strong relation between baskets and women. Female members of the communities bear them while men hunt, and when a woman dies her last burden basket is burnt with her in a special ritual.

But, early in history, humans not only found similarities between things they saw in nature, but also between nature and themselves. For example, the roots of the mandrake, a plant belonging to the same family as tomatoes, bears a striking resemblance to the human body. Because of this, it was believed to be both curative and poisonous throughout history. The 'doctrine of signatures', developed in the 1st century ACE, asserted that plants that had a similarity with a part of the body could be used to cure it. This belief extended in time, and the famous James Joyce novel *Ulysses* (1922) makes reference to it. The main character, Stephen

Dedalus, walks along the beach while saying *"Signatures of all things I am here to read, seaspawn and seawrack, the nearing tide, that rusty boot"*.

The mandrake, like many other plants, had a power over those who merely touched it, causing dizziness, slow heartbeat and difficulty breathing, and could kill those who ingested it – something easily explainable through science, given its alkaloid content. In fact, the plant was believed to be akin to a woman and screamed loudly if anyone attempted to pull it out of the ground. It was particularly popular in the Middle Ages, when it was used in rituals. Amulets were also created by carving the roots, and their association to witchcraft did not go unnoticed to the Catholic Church, which classed the plant as devilish and banned its traditional use.

It is obvious that the strong link between plants and the human body goes beyond physical similarities, and it is actually a reflection of the effects that plants have on human health. Plants have been used since the beginning of time not just to cure ailments as we have already seen, but also to achieve altered states of consciousness that allowed humans to overcome the barriers of their own bodies. In doing so, human groups – or specifically designated people within those groups, such as shamans and chiefs – were able to transcend this world and communicate with other worlds. These leaders are believed to have a deep knowledge of herbs and plants and the ability to connect with spirits through their use. For example, via a totem-like object called *rehue*, the *machi*, the religious leader of the mapuche people of the centre and south of Chile and southwest of Argentina, is said to be able to make contact with friendly spirits and ask them for advice. The *rehue* is actually the representation of the cosmic tree, so plants have a physical, essential role in establishing this connection between different worlds. The totem often features a human face at the top, and is, of course, made of a tree trunk rooted in the ground. Many cultures believe that disease comes from an imbalance between natural and supernatural forces, and plants, through their properties, have a fundamental role in restoring this equilibrium.

Not only do different cultures associate plants to human shape, but also to physiological characteristics. For example, sap from trees often has a milk-like appearance, both in texture and colour. Previously, we mentioned that, for Egyptians, humans needed to be fed milk in the afterlife as if they were children, and women, cows and snakes could fulfil this role. For the Aztecs, there was actually a tree that gave out milk, the *Chichihuacuauhco*, or 'udder tree', which was used to feed forever those children that had died.

The Olmeca people, for example, a culture from the Gulf of Mexico (1600–350 BCE), used plants to communicate with the spirits, predict the future and understand challenging events, such as bad harvests and epidemics.

Different traditions actually highlight the important role that plants have for ecosystems, and since ancestral times cultures developed stories that reminded people of how essential it was to maintain this order. For example, the *guambianos*, in the south of Colombia, made sure that people did not pull the *yas* plant (scientific name, *Brugmansia*) by telling the story of a large bird that lived in it and would punish them if they did so. It seems no wonder that, as this kind of oral tradition gets lost in vast parts of the planets, respect for the environment dwindles. Even in cultures that depend strongly on natural resources, loss of tradition has resulted in polluting the very environments that they need to survive. For example, in recent years, the Bajau people, whose survival depends on fishing, have been throwing all the plastic waste they generate into the very waters they need to keep clean if they want to feed their families. These incredible inhabitants from the coast of Indonesia, the Philippines and Malaysia are often classed as 'superhumans' because of their outstanding ability to dive to 40 metres and to hold their breath under water for 10 minutes. They developed this skill as an answer to their environment, with a diet completely focused on the fish they caught masterfully using large harpoons. Their bodies adapted to their surroundings through the development of larger spleens, which enabled them to have more oxygen in their blood while diving. The story of the Bajau highlights that, no matter the physical adaptations that human groups develop to their environments, there is an essential pool of culturally transmitted knowledge that needs to be preserved if we want this planet to keep being a liveable place for years to come.

Soil and plants link humans to the world, and language is the vehicle which enables us to understand, express and pass that connection onto other humans and down through generations. The universe of words which describe a people's environment is so rich and important; it is a fundamental piece in the preservation of those surroundings. And this connection is also true for the seas: researchers from the universities of Edinburgh and Newcastle in the UK, found out that Scots Gaelic, a language once widely spoken in Scotland and which declined through the 20th century, was particularly preserved in the Outer Hebrides. The population of these islands, whose main means of subsistence is fishing, find in their mother tongue an essential way of passing on all knowledge related to sea activity and product processing. This is an actual phenomenon described by social scientists as 'traditional ecological knowledge', whereby parents teach their children crucial information to navigate their environment. But this precious language pool goes beyond that: it also denotes the community's respect for the sea and all its living organisms, and the tools necessary to make use of it in a sustainable way by not fishing in certain areas and avoiding specific specimens on the basis of their species or age, all of them meticulously described by Scots Gaelic. If this language was lost, this centenary tradition of sustainable fishing would be lost.

Plants, cereals and fibres help us subsist so many ways. We share the land with them, just as we do with animals, and in the next chapter we will see quite how much they also mean for us, both practically and symbolically.

Chapter 3: Born from animals

Animals are incredible creatures. From the beginning of our history, humans used their meat to feed themselves and their fur to protect their bodies from the cold, as well as to build shelters. Later on, humans also started drinking their milk. They were so important for survival, that it is no wonder they transcended their practical aspect and became a fundamental part of human imagination and a central piece of belief and societal systems. It is also no surprise that they were the subject of the first figurative artistic representations. With just a few strokes, our ancestors were able to represent the animals around them, and they cleverly made use of the bumps and creeks in walls to model their physical characteristics. Animals have thus always been a fundamental part of human expression of thoughts and feelings and served art well in every form. In fact, the first ever musical instrument we know appears to be a 60,000-year-old bone flute found in Slovenia, made from the thigh bone of a young bear, and featuring four pierced holes. Although, as we saw in the previous chapter, there could have been previous ones made from reeds.

So-called catgut, which actually came from sheep and goats and not from cats, were fibres found in the intestines of these animals and that are documented to have been used to make strings for instruments since ancient times. Pigs' bladders would have been used since Antiquity for instruments such as bagpipes thanks to their flexibility, which allowed them to be filled with air and retain their shape. Other instrument parts, such as drumheads, were extensively made of animal hides all the way to the 20th century of our era.

If it is creativity we are talking about, we cannot of course forget that animal skin was also the basis of a qualitative and quantitative jump in knowledge which would forever change the world. Books are probably the most illustrative example of how earth, plants and animals are interconnected, and how all organic things have always been and continue to be essential for practical and creative human development.

As explained, the first writing support were tablets, made of clay. Then, Egyptians took a leap by learning how to modify the papyrus plant in order to create a more flexible and larger writing surface. But what really pushed book production was the development of parchments in the Greek city of Pergamum in the 2nd century of the Christian era. By stretching, cleaning and treating the surface of cattle skin, they revolutionised the world of writing and reading. It was a laborious process, and many animals died in the making. But their invention was the most common writing support in Europe until the 14th century, when paper replaced it because it was easier to produce in large quantities. This is exactly what the printing press, invented in that century, required. However, by then, the skin of calves, goats and sheep had served for centuries as the canvas where illuminated manuscripts containing a wealth of knowledge were spread across the world. The essential legacy of this era has survived in our vocabulary: the spine of a book is so called because it corresponded to the middle of the animal's skin, where the mark of the spinal cord could be seen.

The ancient Egyptians gave so much importance to animals, they divinised many of them. They observed nature keenly and found parallels, for example, between the balls made by dung beetles and the rising sun. Their physical appearance and their qualities made them a central part of religious explanations of the world around them, as well as giving them a practical role. For example, the female hippopotamus, with her large belly, was the goddess Taweret, a protector of pregnant women, births and infants. Bastet, the cat, had an essential role in an agricultural society: she had the power of getting rid of pests, a key part of harvest success. Animals such as the cow, the snake and the lioness, had fundamental roles in the Egyptian imagination. And even less well-known ones, like the genet (a cat-like carnivore) or unassuming, like the shrew, were brought to divine level.

No doubt, animals in ancient Egypt were given a divine status because were a fundamental part of everyday life and work. Of course, they were essential to carry out, for example, the ploughing of the fields, but they were also greatly appreciated as domestic companions. We can easily tell how much they enjoyed pets from the ancient Egyptian tomb scenes in which cats happily lie under the chairs of their owners.

Animals were so important for the ancient Egyptians, that they mummified them as offerings. Their correct passing to the afterlife was as essential as that of humans, which prompted Egyptians to mummify animals as small as scarab beetles, just because of their symbolical relevance.

Humans have always admired animal qualities and have sought to acquire them or even transform themselves into them fully through various rituals. All cultures, from the ancient

Egyptians and Greeks and their myths to French writer Voltaire and the Enlightenment, have made use of animals to develop a different self. Whether to hide embarrassing behaviour or to give themselves special powers, individuals relied on animal transformation to do whatever they wanted. Animals actually appear to have served a further purpose, and they were used to criticise society and politics and to reflect on human nature. An extremely well preserved ancient Egyptian papyrus from the 12th-13th century BCE, depicts animals imitating human activities. Interestingly, these creatures also go against their natural instinct. The lion does not attack the gazelle but plays board games with it instead, and goats and geese are peacefully shepherded by hyenas and foxes, amongst others. These scenes appear to be criticising the failure of rulers and judges to keep Maat, which was the name that Egyptians gave the order of the universe, and whose preservation was essential. The balance between opposites that complemented each other was central to that order, as was already explained in the first part of the book. As such, donkeys that appear to be imparting judgment seem to be a less than subtle way of expressing how the artist felt about the ruling class. Other features of the upper class, such as entertainment ensembles used at parties, did not escape this criticism either, and were caricaturised as dancing and singing animals. Further members of the upper classes, such as priests, were also subject to this treatment, as scenes found on ostraca in various sites depict dogs in priestly clothes that mimicked priestly attitudes, presumably with not very positive undertones.

So, humans have always considered animals as the givers of essential food and shelter and their companions in nature, and these fundamental practical roles led them to become an important part of artistic expression and philosophical thought. But not all their roles were so metaphysical, others were more ordinary: animal excrements were essential for agricultural societies, as they made great fertiliser. Even nowadays, they continue to be a sustainable alternative to chemical fertilisers. However, they also have their downsides in terms of pollution, and we will see these pros and cons in more detail and how we can make the most out of animal dung in the Closing the Organic Cycle section.

Vivifying liquid

The topic of whether breastfeeding is best for babies is a recurrent one, with some people thinking nothing can substitute motherly milk and others maintaining that there are formulas nowadays which are just as good and which can provide all the necessary nutrients when, for whatever reason, personal or medical, breastfeeding is not an option. In ancient times, of course, there was no such option, and in Egypt breast milk was considered so essential and vivifying that it was even a fundamental part of reviving the deceased so they could start their lives again in the afterlife. Milk was so important as a liquid in life and death that cows were also strongly associated to motherhood because of their milk production abilities. Certain vessels, shaped as cows or with bovine features, were both present in a domestic sphere and offered to the deceased, who was being born to the other life, as a means of nourishment.

Hathor, the goddess cow, was one of the most important ones in the ancient Egyptian pantheon throughout history. Funnily enough, another animal, which was obviously not a mammal, was also suggested to have breasts. Against all odds, this was the snake. It turns out that establishing a link between snakes and cows is recurrent in agricultural societies: both tend to shelter in the warmth of barns, creating the popular belief that cows actually provide adders with food.

In fairness, snakes were considered divine by ancient Egyptians on their own merits. Their godly status probably came from their link to agriculture. Snakes are very common in stables and therefore live close to rural houses, being seen as a symbol of prosperity and fertility of the fields. They were thus considered protective and had renewal abilities. This idea, as so many others, extended into the afterlife; since this was an extension of earthly life, agricultural production also had to be guaranteed after death. That would explain the association between milk and snakes, as both were protective and had life-giving properties.

In addition, snakes have a series of physical features, such as white saliva, stomach contents and skin colour in some cases, which could have also been the reason why people believed these animals produced milk.

However, far from being exclusive to ancient Egypt, the link between snakes, cows and the feminine sphere is present in many cultures, with numerous legends associating snakes to bovines and women because of the latter's milk production and feeding abilities. In its simplest form, these oral traditions claim that snakes are attracted to cow's milk. Even nowadays, in India and Nepal, snakes have the privilege of being offered ritual milk as part of colourful rituals in festivals such as Nag Panchami.

Even more widespread are the legends that say that snakes are attracted to human milk, and that they even fight babies for it. In some versions, the cunning snakes go as far as sticking their tail into the baby's mouth to prevent them from crying because of losing their food. In Guanajuato, in Mexico, they know a fair bit about this. Local folklore says that a certain type of snake, called *alicante*, takes advantage of any moment when a breastfeeding mother dozes off to suckle from their breast. From the Iberian Peninsula to the American continent, similar legends abound that justify women losing their ability to produce milk.

As both cow and human milk were recognised to have such nourishing properties, it is only natural that they also played an important part in ancient Egyptian medicine. If you fell ill in ancient Egypt, you were likely to improve if you drank milk, but you were also likely to use this liquid to take whatever other medicine was necessary, though wine or honey could also help you in this task. In other cases, breast milk could provide medical information about the patient, and features extensively in medicine treaties. In a remedy which seems curious to us to say the least, a woman who wanted to check her fertility had to drink the milk of a woman who had conceived a child; if she vomited it, it meant she was or would soon be pregnant.

But the power of milk and its links with snakes or snake-like organisms does not end there. African-American folk medicine, recommends that, to eliminate tapeworm, the patient must lie with his mouth facing a bowl of milk. Being attracted by the milk, the tapeworm will leave the body.

Other remedies require a more intense interaction from the patient, and they cut it short by directly immersing themselves in the vivifying liquid that is milk.

Milk is believed, of course, to have softening properties for the skin, and Cleopatra was famously said to bathe in donkey milk. However, cosmetic improvements were not the only thing that milk could do for you. Milk could also help you transform from human into animal. In English and Scottish legends such as that of Tam Lin (documented at least from 1549), immersion in milk was a fundamental part of being human again after having been turned into an animal, and vice versa.

But animals did not just provide a by-product to help ailments, they were themselves the actual treatment. If medical texts do not shy away from the properties of the natural liquid, tomb scenes show us the vivifying powers of a good feast: cows' heads and legs, ducks that have seen better days, all were able to magically come to life to feed the deceased for eternity.

Under the skin

You might have heard of 'glamping', a glamorous alternative which aims to offer urbanites the experience of camping, while avoiding the discomforts of living amongst nature in a temporary shelter. But for many human groups across history, making a suitable home for themselves in a temporary or semi-temporary structure was a fundamental part of their community life and subsistence practices. And as always, organic materials were a key part of achieving this comfortable home, which was often also a place of gathering with other members of the group.

Nomadic people of the Asian steppe have used large circular tents since they can remember. Their main activity is as herders and hunters, and depending on the time of the season, they need to move with their herds in search of other areas that provide the necessary amount of food to their animals. When they move, they take their houses with them, so these need to be light enough to be transported. Almost as if to thank them, the sheep provide the wool that the herders use to build their tents. They beat the wool to crush it, and this naturally binds the material and creates a solid felt.

The sheep's role in housing does not end there. Thanks to their milk or fat, the nomads are able to make the felt's surface waterproof and provide insulation for the tents. This fabric lies over a wooden lattice framework, with a hole at the top that allows light to get in and smoke to come out. Everything is carefully thought out in the yurt, as these tents are called, and even the top can be used to cure the cheese they make. Not everything has to be practical though, and the outer walls can be embellished with embroidery representations of local fauna and flora.

As is usually the case with traditional houses, these are often preserved mainly for tourism, although they are still frequent in places such as the Gobi Desert; some of them have been combined with modern innovations, such as solar panels!

Similar to the yurts, the *itchalik*, the traditional dome-shaped tent of the Nunamiut Eskimos in Alaska, make use of animal by-products to cover a structure made of wooden poles. These wooden poles are traditionally made of willow trees, and this group prefers young specimens, with fewer branches, because they provided strength to the structure. The only difference is that the

Nunamiut use caribou (reindeer) animal skin instead of wool as walls for their homes, but the components of both were as easily transported to another location. In the case of the *itchalik*, women sew the animal hides together in various panels, with the furry side looking out. The caribou skin is also a great insulation material, as the hollow hairs help trap the air. But to add yet more protection, another hairless layer was added on top of the first one, and then the layers were sewn together.

The Nunamiut went even further when it came to making use of the resources in their surroundings to provide the best housing conditions. They used bear intestines or seal guts to create a translucent window, and by doing that, they managed to have natural light inside the tent. And so as not to spoil the cold and wind protection provided by the caribou walls, the door opening was covered by a large bear hide.

But, with temperatures of between -17 and -45 degrees Celsius in the winter, the Nunamiut tents needed all the warmth they could get, and this was most important in the sleeping area. The floor itself was made from caribou hides, and each mattress was also made of a young caribou hide, and calf and cow skins used as blankets.

Another example of the way in which animal skin has traditionally been used to provide shelter is the tepee, which probably became familiar to Western audiences through Hollywood western movies, no matter how many cultural misconceptions about Native people these films include. In fact, probably one of these misgivings was to portray tepees as the only Native American traditional dwelling, when in reality a range of different ones existed, amongst them, some made with earth. But tepees shared with yurts and *itchalik* the convenience of being able to be pulled apart and transported easily. In this case, it was buffalo skins that were sewn over a framework of wooden poles, and even reed mats, bark sheets and others could be used as cover.

Throughout history and whether in earth, plant or animal form, or a combination of any of those elements, humans have made the most of nature for the basic need of shelter. But, at some point, humans also felt that clothing was essential, and animals were ready once again to fulfil yet another essential role.

In sheep's clothing

As already mentioned, animals would have played an essential part in providing humans with clothing, particularly before the development of textiles. At some point during the Palaeolithic period, probably over a million years ago, our ancestors would have started wearing clothes. In time, portable insulation would have been needed, and for that they had to modify animal skins to make them a more convenient fit. Other parts of animals were also involved in this process: their bones helped make tools such as pointed awls and needles with which it was possible to turn animal hides into fitted garments with sleeves and leggings.

We cannot underestimate how important this was for humans, as during the coldest stage of the last ice age, outfits appeared with different layers which protected them from the cold and the wind and allowed us to get to the Arctic Circle. By at least 15,000 years ago, they could have entered the Americas for the first time. The find of a 13,000-year-old eyed needle in Alaska proves the point that sewing was a very important change that enabled movement. A further clue as to the potential relation between sewn clothes and cold is that, according to prehistorian Ian Gilligan, in periods when environmental conditions are warmer, tools such as needles tend to disappear from the archaeological record.

Then, 12,000 years ago, the weather changed again. Temperatures raised, continental ice sheets melted and sea levels rose, which led to a more humid environment that suited fabric clothing better. Woven garments would have allowed a degree of ventilation. These changes would have favoured the development of textile clothing, aided (some even think it would have been the other way around) by the beginning of agriculture.

But plant fibres were not the only thing that could be woven, and we have evidence from statues from Iran that wool garments would have been worn at least since 6000 BCE.

In time, a fabric derived from animals even became so prestigious it had its own trade route: it was silk. Incredibly, this luxurious fabric, which prompted travels across the world, originated from something as small as the cocoons of worms.

A trade as smooth as silk

The Silk Road connected East Asia to Europe, India and Africa, providing not just luxury garments, but also decorative textiles, as well as a writing support. The actual earliest sample of woven silk dates from ca 2700 BCE, in the site of Qianshanyang, in China. By the second millennium BCE, it was being produced on a large scale, and then traded with other parts of the world, such as Egypt, where Chinese silk dated to ca 1600–1046 BCE has been found. The looms used to create the silk fabric feature in the murals of the tombs of the Han dynasty (206 BCE–220 CE). The silk could then be dyed and painted using natural pigments, such as those coming from clam shells and various plants like indigo.

In the first century of the Christian era, the techniques got even more sophisticated, and the growth of worms was controlled by adjusting the temperature of their environment. In time, breeds were even mixed to create different textures. It was considered such a precious textile that its colour and embroidery became a status symbol, and in some cases, like Korea, there were even rules about the lower classes not being able to wear it.

Women were a central part of the silk industry, as it was their job to guarantee the comfort and feeding conditions of the worms and they were usually in charge of weaving. Eventually, the manufacturing spread to other countries such as Korea and Japan, India, Byzantium and beyond.

Its value was such that bolts of silk were used as currency in China in the 10th and 11th century by traders, and to pay tributes and even armies.

Once again, an animal sourced material became closely associated to art, with silk being used to paint landscape scenes and portraits. It brought great sophistication to the book scene, as it was even used to create pages on which famous paintings were copied.

The Silk Road not only permitted the back-and-forth movement of this precious textile, but it also allowed for language and writing to be spread, as well as ideas such as Buddhism and Christianity. It also meant that new food, such as coriander, sesame and pomegranates arrived in China. It made the world richer and more connected, and all through the threads of a tiny animal that many would have dismissed.

Never a hair out of place

Hair has been a fundamental part of people's identities across time and cultures. It has been seen not just as a symbol of femininity, but as a source of power for everyone. An example that will be familiar to some people is that of Samson, a character from the Bible whose superhuman strength derived from his hair. Just as clothing, hair and hairdos have also been a way of expressing social status across history.

Seeing how important it was both for defining individual identity and social class, it is no wonder that people grew it and styled it in different ways. What might be more surprising to hear is that humans have also added to their own hair since Antiquity, and that extensions were already a thing in ancient Egypt. The earliest example of ancient Egyptian hair extensions is a set of natural braids discovered in a female temple in a necropolis in Hierakonpolis, in such a good state of preservation it is hard to believe they are over 5,000 years old.

In case anyone doubts that these could have been used as proper hair extensions, the evidence is in a relief from the 11th dynasty (ca 2008–1957 BCE) which depicts Queen Neferu and is currently in the Brooklyn Museum. The fragment of limestone, originally belonging to a larger scene, shows the queen's hairdresser styling the royal hair by pinning one strand of hair after another, as well as twisting another strand. Another fragment of the same relief depicts another hairdresser ready to place a triple lock of hair on the queen's head.

If additional hair strands and locks gave a different look to their wearer, an even more dramatic transformation was that enabled by wigs. Wigs were extensively used and found highly convenient for different reasons, worn both by men and women. Temples even featured hairdressing workshops where these wigs were made. As these were more costly and time-consuming to make than mere extensions, they would have probably been used only by the elite.

The most peculiar aspect of wigs is that they were not just cosmetic accessories, but they also had a practical function. It was not uncommon for certain members of society, such as priests, to shave off their heads. By wearing a wig, shaved heads could be protected from the sun and from head lice, a frequent companion of natural hair in certain conditions. In fact, these wigs were built on a mesh, so ventilation was guaranteed.

As we have now seen time and again, organic substances from different sources came together to enhance the object and make it perform its role more efficiently. In this case, beeswax and resin were spread on human hair to help fix it to the mesh. These natural substances were an extremely efficient glue in Egypt's high temperatures. Then, about 2.5 cm of each strand was looped around the foundation and glued again to the wax on the hair strand.

Needless to say, the ancient Egyptians were not the last ones to use human hair to make wigs. The Greeks and the Romans also used them, and it saw a revival in the 16th century, again to assist with parasites while asserting social position, although some records from the 17th century bear witness to the fact that the human hair used to make these wigs could also come complete with parasites from its previous owner.

Wigs made of human hair continue to be an important feature of many people's lives even nowadays, especially those who have lost their hair because of medical conditions or treatments. Across the world, people of all ages purposely grow their hair long so they can donate the hair to charities that make wigs for people that require them, and this endless organic source is likely to continue to help other people for years to come.

Under the sea

Have you ever lost a small object you held very dear and how far would you go to retrieve it? Many objects such as pendants went beyond their decorative purposes in ancient Egypt; they also acted as amulets, so losing them could badly affect a person's luck. It was so important that an ancient Egyptian story in the so-called Westcar papyrus tells us that a magician recovered a woman's lost pendant by moving half of the water of the lake she was rowing in onto the other half. The young woman, who was one of the king's rowers, dropped a turquoise fish ornament that was hanging off the end of her braid. The king offered to replace it, but it must have had a great personal value to her, as she would not rest until her own pendant was returned to her.

Fish were actually strongly associated with beauty. They feature frequently as palettes that would have held natural pigments that ancient Egyptians put on as make-up. Although make-up was not exclusive to women, fish do have a strong association with femininity. They represent fertility and rebirth, concepts which were central to the ancient Egyptian universe, as has been remarked throughout the book.

One of the reasons why this link was established was a fish commonly found in the Nile at the time, called tilapia. The tilapia had the peculiarity of incubating eggs in its mouth. When the fish were ready to be born, it opened its mouth and they were released into the water. But this hide could also work the other way around: if the fish encountered some danger, they could take refuge again in their mother's mouth until the hazard had passed, a time when they were released again. Imagine the impact this had on ancient Egyptians, who were such great observers of their environment. A fish that gave life, swallowed its children back, then gave them life again! It is easy to see how this common observation turned into a powerful regeneration symbol for them.

Of course, the association of fish with life continued to be relevant later in history, and the first Christians used the fish as a symbol of Jesus and therefore of his resurrection. This symbolism is found in many examples across the New Testament, such as the multiplication of the loaves and fish.

Real examples of turquoise fish pendants such as the one described in the story of the king's rower have reached us, and it is understandable that such colour was used to evoke water, though other precious metals, such as gold, were also used. Though precious stones and metals are more frequent, organic materials were also used to depict fish, and we have examples of terracotta figures of tilapias with their characteristic pouting lips, which often lend themselves to being used as spouts for cosmetic containers.

For ancient Egypt, we are lucky enough to have objects and also depictions of how these were born. It is thanks to a small sculpture of a girl supporting a pot, which actually serves as a cosmetic container, that we know that these pendants were hung off the end of plaits. What is even more striking is that this sculpture also gives us information about other sea creatures that were born decoratively: the girl has a girdle depicting cowrie (a sea snail) shells, real strung examples of which we actually can find in the archaeological record.

Sea life continues to be associated with beauty nowadays. It is believed to have incredible hydrating, repairing and anti-ageing properties, so it is no wonder that some of the most expensive moisturizing face creams in the market have seaweed as their main ingredient. There are plenty of recipes on the Internet to make seaweed face masks by mixing it with clay and water. As much as we might find it annoying when we swim on the beach, it is an essential part of many coastal ecosystems, as it absorbs CO_2. Luckily, there are farms where algae can be grown sustainably without removing it from necessary places. Algae are another example of the incredible versatility of organic materials we have seen so far. Beauty treatments are by no means their only purpose, as they can be used as food and food wrapping and to make packaging, biofuel and even clothes, as we will see in part II.

A natural progression

Over the course of part I we have attempted to paint a picture of the many ways in which organic materials are, and continue to be, an essential part of human existence. Through ancient objects, contemporary human group artefacts and stories and even just a reflection about our own surroundings and traditions, we have come to realise just how much earth, plants and animals are still part of our everyday life, wherever we live. We have seen that, beyond being merely practical, organic objects are so fundamental to our lives that they are deeply embedded into our traditions, into the stories we tell about ourselves and about others.

We are at a crucial crossroad for our planet: while we dismiss essential, millenary knowledge as old-fashioned and unscientific, consequently losing it, we also seek answers for previously answered questions we have chosen to ignore. We can preserve that treasure trove of information before it is too late and make use of modern technology to communicate traditions and solutions. We can also combine such knowledge with the latest technological advances to provide the most sustainable answers to our current climate issues. We certainly need the youngest generations, who are much more concerned about the planet than previous ones, to make that change, but we also need to connect them to a former – sometimes current – way of living which relied heavily on oral tradition, community engagement and folklore. Part II of this book will attempt to suggest ways in which we can not only apply sustainable solutions to our lives, but also learn from those who encountered such problems before us.

Part II: Rebirth

Climate change is undeniable. There is plenty of scientific evidence supporting the fact that our environment is undergoing dramatic changes that affect every being in nature in one way or another, whether plants, animals or humans. Resources are becoming rapidly depleted, and it is always the already weakest links of the chain that suffer the most. It was this situation, paired with a weariness and, often, rejection of mass consumerism, that first led some people to think of ways in which we could slow down consumption. Needless to say, it was a trend developed in western areas, in places where basic needs, such as food and dress, were already covered for a large proportion (not the whole) of the population, so that attention could be turned to issues beyond basic day-to-day survival.

In the 1990s we started worrying about the number of trees that needed felling in order to provide all the paper for our supermarket receipts, or to print out letters and marketing flyers. Recycled paper, with its yellowy tone and irregular texture, unnerved and excited people in equal measure. As emails and Internet files replaced traditional paper documents, people saw the need to add a little icon of a tree at the end of their electronic correspondence advising the recipient to 'only print out this message if necessary'.

The environment awareness trend continued through the 2000s, as more and more Western cities started prompting their inhabitants to recycle and to separate waste for processing at home (sometimes enforcing this practice through fines). While most people had spent all their lives throwing eggshells, bottles or wrappings into a big black bin, they were now encouraged to use separate containers for organic waste, plastic and paper.

In recent years, there has been a qualitative step: a surge of businesses focused on the concept of zero waste. If your online search history shows even a mild concern for the environment, you are likely to have seen adverts for bamboo toothbrushes, charcoal toothpaste or reusable straws pop up here and there while you read the digital paper or do some online shopping.

The concept of zero carbon houses pre-dates that of zero waste. The idea is to create self-sustainable houses, which consume only the same or less amount of energy they created. What seems a perfectly reasonable idea is not always as easy to implement as one would like. Culture plays an important role; in some countries, like Spain, for example, it is difficult to convince people that a long-term investment in solar panels makes perfect sense for a country with areas that enjoy 320 days of sunshine a year. Many people think they might be dead by the time they get a return on that money. It is not just cultural factors that prevent sustainable approaches to housing being commonplace: very often authorities give little compensation for such efforts, or even tax them.

The origins of the zero-waste movement are interesting. The first book published on it was by Bea Johnson, who decided to try and reduce her yearly waste to what fitted inside a small jar, turning it into a symbol of the zero waste goals. The journey is not exempt of contradictions (like when the author says that she used to drive long distances to be able to buy food in bulk and free of plastic packaging). Some tips will hardly come across as epiphanies to some readers, such as the author's suggestion to replace paper serviettes with fabric napkins; to make it work, everyone in the family must keep an identifying ring around it so that they can reuse it for several days (something which I always did in my family home, sometimes the napkins matched the tablecloth, most often they did not). It is not the only product that sounds familiar: suggestions include make-up pads being replaced by flannels, and Tupperware by wax paper, both things an ordinary feature of many people's childhoods. Refilling milk glass jars or returning lemonade bottles to the shop were common occurrences in many Western countries just a couple of decades ago.

Whilst it is true that Johnson, for example, acknowledges having grown up watching parents who constantly repaired and recycled things in their own way, it seems to me that not enough environmental proposals establish a connection with the way things were done in the past. They do sometimes even less so with the way other cultures have traditionally provided solutions to storage and product transformation. The reference to the past is a way to legitimise, almost anecdotally, the usefulness of the product, i.e. "Romans already used charcoal toothpaste". It does not engage with the history and circumstances of the organic product, whether in the past or in contemporary societies. It is obvious that just because something was used by an ancient society, it does not mean it is suitable anywhere and everywhere. But, at the same time, the lessons that come from studying our past, and from being aware of other societies' mores beyond our own Western society, are endless. For that reason, understanding the geographical and cultural connections of the objects or materials is crucial to determining whether they can help us achieve a more sustainable society, whilst also maintaining the current standards of health. Was/is there a usefulness to it which can be demonstrated? Or was/is it believed to be useful for reasons which are not necessarily empirically verifiable, such as religious or cultural associations? Was/is it used because there was no other option available? If its use was eventually discontinued, what was the reason? These are all questions we need to ask ourselves if we want to reach an understanding of the ways in which organic materials have played, and can continue to play, a role in our lives.

The most shocking thing of it all is that so often we try to find solutions for problems while at the same time destroying or ignoring the answers available to us. Any efficient and long-lasting solution to tackle climate change and global food challenges must combine tradition with the new knowledge and technology available. It must be brought about globally, through the combination of thousands of local solutions. It requires thinking of what communities around the world have in common, but also what makes them different and how they can use these peculiarities towards building common answers.

It is precisely this concept of community that is at the centre of the whole idea, and what more often than not fails in a world where communication is easier than ever, but where global initiatives often get hindered by bureaucracy and financial interests. The concept of community as a small-scale group, with its own internal web of emotional and productive relations and dependencies, has also become gradually degraded by factors such as national and international migration. Following the unprecedented disruption of habits caused by COVID across the world, there is an opportunity to rethink these trends and align them with climate change and global development solutions. Resource control is also a major source of conflict, so these agreements are also a key factor in fostering peaceful relations between regions.

Chapter 1: Have your veg and eat it

Food production and consumption is one of the areas that has been most affected by the replacement of traditional methods and local know-how for a one-size-fits-all approach designed to fit artificial market demands. Overexploitation of land and resources at a massive scale has, of course, a dramatic impact on sustainability. Time and again, ecosystems are destroyed because of excessive cultivation, sometimes motivated by need, but often by greed. Overdevelopment is also at the centre of human tragedy related to climate change, as floods and fires affect areas where buildings should have never existed. Of course, many people are forced to live in these inconvenient locations, driven by ridiculously high prices in safe areas. But the building industry has been, for decades, exhausting areas and dramatically affecting their biodiversity in the name of urban expansion, often in the search of tourism income, amongst others. Spain is a prime example of this, with excessive developments being built right next to the sea, on cliffs that now are slowly eroding due to climate and weather changes. The Mar Menor beaches, in the southeast coast of Spain, have repeatedly had to be closed to the public after being deemed unsafe for swimming. The waters of this unique lagoon ecosystem were so dirty that, for several years, thousands of fish have turned up dead at the shore due to lack of oxygen. But excessive tourism and building are not the only cause behind this situation; the excessive use of fertilisers which filtrate through the soil and get into water bodies has also caused contamination and deoxidation, killing sea life. To this, we must add that this is an area which is already sensitive to climate change and where water resources are already stretched due to the large proliferation of golf courses and resorts, again aimed at attracting wealthy tourists.

Therefore, as the Barilla Food and Nutrition Centre points out, the focus of any changes in food production and consumption must be centred around serving human needs whilst maintaining the diversity and stability of natural ecosystems. Changing the food production system requires thinking of innovative solutions, such as permaculture, which allows for maximisation of food production while minimising labour. But changes in production must be paired with changes in consumption. As we previously saw, fads about superfoods put an unnecessary stress on production systems, as does the availability of seasonal foods all year around and the meat industry. However, the search for new foods to eat does not have to be detrimental, as diversifying the vegetables consumed can actually help relieve the stress on particular foods. There are many means of food preservation which allow for sustainable consumption, and food forests greatly help the environment whilst providing food.

The thing is, many of these are practices with a long tradition in many societies, which have been passed on from generation to generation orally. This information, combined with innovation in food production, is paramount to achieve global sustainability goals. For example, the food forest of Inraren in Morocco is an incredible place where, for centuries, people have cultivated the most convenient species, mimicked nature's symbiosis between different ones and progressively created a self-sufficient 'natural supermarket' where everything they need is at hand. Traditional practices such as no-till or low-till farming do not disturb the soil and increase water retention, preventing erosion. Soil is healthier through it, with crop waste remaining on the surface and water not getting evaporated or running off. By using natural fertilisers and pesticides, pollution is avoided. Not only that, but a healthier soil is better prepared to withstand the effects of climate change, such as floods or draughts.

As well as using traditional ways of cultivation, another recommendation is diversifying agriculture; growing a broader range of species helps tackle pests and climate and market changes. This could be achieved by combining annual and perennial plants, as well as planting trees and agricultural crops together, a millenary practice called 'agroforestry'. And it works both ways, as trees can feature in plants, but also farming can be done in forests or along their margins. The benefits, according to Tony Simons, director general of the World Agroforestry Centre (ICRAF), are more nutritious and resistant crops. Conversely, the wood and fruits from trees can be used to feed animals, for fuel and for building barns. Shorter and taller plants can be combined, such as coconut trees and banana trees, as well as edible shrubs and groundcover. Planting in this way also helps prevent erosion and water evaporation.

Rice is one of the main crops to tackle. According to the Food and Land Use Coalition, it is consumed everyday by 3.5 billion people and over 1 billion people's livelihoods depend on its production. Rice has a severe impact in the ecosystems where it is cultivated, as it releases large amounts of methane. In addition, bad practices have severely affected mangroves and forests.

Through using the aforementioned agricultural methods, it is possible to reduce methane emissions by 70% and make use of those landscapes as carbon sinks and biodiversity hubs.

This can be paired up with new attitudes towards food consumption. For example, drawing on people's family experiences and memories, the Free Tree Society in Kuala Lumpur gathered stories about food in periods of hardship, unveiling a whole load of seeds, weeds and leaves that people used to consume in the 1940s.

But given the perishable nature of food, sustainability is also about food reuse. According to the FAO (Food and agriculture organisation of the United Nations), one-third of food produced for human consumption is lost or wasted globally, which amounts to about 1.3 billion tonnes per year. Faced with this reality, it is essential to think creatively about ways in which this food can be repurposed, either for further consumption or for other uses. For example, International Flavours Fragrances collects spinach waste (vegetables which are not deemed good enough to be sent to the supermarket) and effectively uses new technology to turn it into a powder which they incorporate into snack bars and nutrient drinks. Through an infrared technique, they are able to dry fruit and vegetables into reusable powder, with the advantage of keeping their nutrients and taste.

There are also a range of apps available whose aim is to stop restaurants throwing out food and to tell you where you can collect food across the city, often at a discounted price. Not everybody supports the initiative though, as it ends up creating a market for something that otherwise could be donated to charity, as indeed some restaurants do.

A real tyranny of food production is that referred to fruit and vegetables that do not meet the expected aesthetic standards. Fruits like apples are not packed if they are not perfectly round, glistening spheres. Luckily, some factories separate those and collaborating businesses use them to make pastry and pies.

The truth is that, as the challenges of feeding a growing world population increase, alternative foods must be considered, and a large amount of research is necessary to provide these options. As previously mentioned, cattle require a large amount of agricultural soil, and there is also the issue of cows largely contributing to methane levels, highly detrimental to the ozone layer. Cattle is also fed by crops, which need large amounts of water and which are deviated from human consumption if used for animals.

Therefore, animal meat is one of the main areas that food research focuses on with the idea of replacing current consumption and changing our future diet. There are different ways in which this can be achieved: by replacing animal meat with plant-based alternatives, by using fermentation and by cultivating meat.

Plant-based meat has existed for centuries, and you might be surprised at hearing that the first mention of tofu, one of the most popular plant-based meat substitutes, is by a Chinese text from 965 of the Christian era. Although we have to wait until the 19th century for the first recorded mention of plant-based meat in the Western world, the truth is that, since that first Chinese text, we have several mentions to wheat gluten being used to replace animal meat.

You have probably seen some plant-based products in your usual supermarket, although they are always outnumbered by real meat products and they have been primarily aimed at vegetarians.

For years, the objective was to provide an alternative to those who did not want to eat animal meat because of ethical reasons, or that had been recommended not to eat meat because of their health. However, in the last decade, sustainability awareness has led many more people to become interested in this type of food, while not necessarily giving up animal products completely. Although the main difference between animals and plants is that the latter do not have muscles, they do have similarities in terms of their composition which help lead them to smell, taste and look similar. Water, minerals, fat, protein and vitamins are components of both plants and animals. But to best reproduce the advantages of animal products in plants, crop cultivation must be optimised, both through traditional and new methods, and the most convenient crop types identified.

Fermentation is a technique which has been used by humans for millennia to preserve and create food and alcoholic drinks. This is the case with lactic acid bacteria, used to make cheese and yoghurt. In modern food technology, fermentation through the use of microorganisms is being seen as a way to create large amounts of protein or make plant-based foods more palatable.

Cultivated meat consists in producing animal meat directly from cells. Instead of the muscle and fat cells developing inside the animal, the animal cells can grow in a cultivator, a bit like using cuttings to develop full plants. It is an efficient way of using the land, avoiding the use of antibiotics and the need for cramming animals into small spaces, although it is yet to be developed at a commercial scale. Its proponents claim that cultivated meat tastes and smells like traditional meat, as it is identical to meat at cellular level. However, the process of cultivating meat can help avoid diseases, deforestation and water use and pollution.

Surprisingly, a food that can be used to create a substitute for bacon is mushrooms. Incredibly, they cannot only be turned into rashers that – at least according to the engineers that developed them – taste very similar to bacon; research is also underway to turn them into a biodegradable material similar to Styrofoam, a plastic-based material used for packaging which is not easily recyclable.

Ultimately, the combination of traditional knowledge with modern technology can help build a sustainable food production system even before crops are planted. Through the use of remote sensing, a drone can fly over fields and identify what the best areas are to plant crops in order to maximise yields. By doing this evaluation before planting, farmers can decide their cultivation patterns and optimise the amount of fertiliser they use, as well as reducing pollution by minimising the amount of time that tractors need to be used.

What can I do, realistically?

While it is hard to influence food production as individuals, we can support the cultivation of organic vegetables and fruits, which avoids the use of harmful pesticides. Although these are often more expensive, the benefits for both the environment and our own health are obvious.

In addition, there is a range of things we can do to improve the efficiency of our food consumption, in a way that reduces food waste while helping our pockets.

Some solutions refer to our shopping habits, while others are to do with the way we store food once we get home. To begin with, while more frequent and smaller shopping trips can be inconvenient in terms of time (and potentially pollution if driving is needed), they have also been proven to be efficient to reduce waste. Some people also find it useful to plan meals weekly.

Once food has reached our home, we must store it in an efficient way. The refrigerator should be kept below 5 ºC, and cooked food placed above raw food. Containers should be appropriate, so avoid using metal cans.

Not long ago, it was commonplace to repurpose everything that entered the kitchen. For example, growing up in Spain, stale bread was often made into breadcrumbs with the help of a hand mincer which was fixed to the kitchen counter with a bolt. Some people still use this to make breadcrumbs for different traditional meals, and it is a great way to reuse bread rather than throwing it. The same goes for frying pieces of bread to use as croutons for soups or salads.

If these methods of reuse are not common where you come from, there are plenty of resources on the Internet that suggest ways in which leftovers and foods that are about to go off can be repurposed. For example, vegetables on the verge of wilting can be used for soups and smoothies. Chicken and bones can be used for stock and soup.

Freezing food is another way of stopping it from going off. For example, you can freeze chopped onion in a container and use it for many months. Another way of preserving foods that wilt particularly easily, such as herbs, is to freeze them in oil cubes. When needed, they can be quickly melted in the pan and repurposed.

Our ancestors used different methods to preserve food, from salting it to pickling it. This can be done with almost any food.

Increasingly, there are calls to use common sense when deciding whether food needs throwing away. The expressions on pre-packed food, such as 'use by', lead people to think food is not safe after that date. A particularly frequent case is that of yoghurts. Recently, some brands of yoghurts available in Europe have started carrying a "smell, look and taste" sign that encourages consumers to check on the product, as often this can be safely eaten for a good number of days – even weeks – after the use by date. By applying these principles sensibly, throwing food unnecessarily can be avoided, though if we are not sure whether food is off it is better to be safe than sorry and dispose of it.

The composition of some food also gives clues as to whether it is still safe to eat. Generally, meat and fish tend to go grey with the effect of excessive air and have a sour taste. However, the state of other food items, such as eggs, cannot be told from their flavour, but luckily there is a popular way of checking. This traditional trick is based on the natural chemical process that occurs when the egg goes off, as gas builds up in it. If we put it in a glass water and it sinks to the bottom, that means there is no gas and we can safely eat it. But if it hovers a bit or floats to the top completely, it means the egg is full of gas and we should avoid consuming it.

Some parts of food are actually good for us and do not need throwing, such as the peel of fruit and vegetables. They contain a lot of nutrients, such as fibre, vitamins and minerals. For example, apple peels contain a compound called triterpenoid, a powerful antioxidant. Other parts, such as pumpkin seeds, can be consumed as snacks when toasted.

Even coffee grounds can be repurposed as fertiliser, and they are high in nutrients plants need, such as potassium, phosphorus and nitrogen, as well as being a powerful tool against mosquitoes.

Many foods can also be used to create face masks and other cosmetic products. Doing so both helps avoid chemical products and allows you to repurpose things like egg, avocado, tea bags and cucumber slices (which can be applied to puffy eyes).

All in all, with the right organisation and attitude, there are plenty of things you can do to start reducing your food waste at home.

Chapter 2: No time to waste

It is not rare for a *National Geographic* magazine cover to become iconic. It happened in 1984, when the picture of a green-eyed Afghan girl firmly staring at the camera became a symbol of the plight of refugees across the world. In 2018 another striking cover was published, this time to do with another pressing topic: climate change.

The cleverly composed photograph appeared to show the tip of an iceberg floating above sea water and a much larger ice mass submerged below. However, a few seconds of looking at it revealed that what seemed like an iceberg was, in reality, a plastic bag floating in the ocean. It worked perfectly on so many levels: it made an immediate association between the environment and plastic, it portrayed an actual physical reality – that plastic floats freely in waters all across the world – and it made a further point about the fact that what we get to see is but 'the tip of the iceberg' of a much bigger and deeper problem.

In fact, one of the challenges about communicating the climate emergency is that changes sometimes occur over a long period of time, which in turn makes individuals perceive them as less severe. It sometimes takes shocking instances of rare weather and unusual phenomena for people to realise how serious a topic climate change is. It is also a global problem, and people can find it difficult to empathise with what happens on the other side of the world or to feel that it affects them in any way. There is also a disconnection between our actions at home and in the street and the general effects on the planet, which is why the *National Geographic* cover was so effective in bringing the topic home by showing a plastic bag that any of us could pick up in a supermarket.

There are plenty of statistics that can be shared about plastic, but numbers and percentages often do not serve their purpose. We become immune to them because our brain brushes over them when we see them, sometimes because we simply find it difficult to comprehend what they mean in practical terms. It is, therefore, a challenge to communicate what we can do about it. There is also often a general feeling that this is a problem that only big corporations can solve, and that individuals have just a tiny impact on the whole thing. This assumption is not entirely wrong – companies do have a massive part to play.

Plastic is a business and, while corporations jump on the bandwagon and enjoy the benefits of making their brand 'green', they are helping spread plastic packaging through their products, or even manufacturing plastic themselves. The problem with ordinary plastic is not just that it takes decades to disappear, it is also that its production process is highly polluting and energy consuming. Some large companies are experimenting with things like cardboard bottles, but until the benefits of producing sustainable packages do not supersede the profits made by producing plastic, corporations will not be getting rid of plastic completely. The worst part is that these brands also spread their plastic packaging in poor areas of the world which do not have the right means to process plastic waste, effectively creating a long-lasting health problem for those communities.

As more research is done, other issues related to plastic emerge which deepen the problem. Although microplastics have been a researchers' concern for the past twenty years, especially in what concerns marine fauna ingesting them, their possible implications for human health have only recently entered the broader public discussion. The size of these small pieces, less than five millimeters long, helps them reach the water bodies easily. Even though the full extent of their damage is still to be determined, these tiny bits of plastic, found in everyday products such as toothpaste, are a big cause of concern due to them being extremely hard to eliminate.

So how can mass plastic consumption be tackled? In the first instance, by eliminating plastic bags and packaging, mostly associated with the food industry. It might seem unthinkable to us, but just 50 years ago, plastic bags were by no means a common product across the world. Originally invented in Sweden in 1959, they quickly spread across Europe and to the United States, and by the end of the 1980s, plastic had almost replaced paper bags all over the globe. Over the following decades, they became ubiquitous not just in every household, but also in every landscape, as their fossil fuel materials meant they took a very long time to degrade. Ireland was the first country to introduce a charge for plastic bags in 2002, which quickly led to a massive reduction in their use. Other countries followed suit, and in 2015, England became the last European country to tax plastic bags. The tax on plastic bags has made customers look for suitable alternatives. Large reusable hard plastic bags are a first step, but there are plenty of other choices which are becoming more and more common, such as knitted net bags.

Also, in 2002, Bangladesh made a bold move when they banned the use of plastic bags completely. Plastic had been responsible for clogging sewerage systems during large floods, and the country became the first in the world to nip the problem in the bud. Since then, countries such as Kenya have also made this important decision for the environment.

A slightly slower issue to tackle, compared to plastic bags, is that of plastic wrapping. As small businesses have been replaced by large supermarkets all across the world – and in some European countries, these local businesses barely exist anymore – polystyrene trays and plastic wrappings have made their way into our homes. But is it really necessary to wrap a piece of fruit in plastic, for example? The answer is no, and the European Union knows this. To fix it, they have drawn some common objectives for state members to reduce the amount of plastic packaging in supermarkets. As a result, French legislation was passed banning the use of plastic for wrapping fruit and vegetables from January 2021 and, in October 2021, Spain followed suit and announced that they would be banning plastic wrapping for groceries from 2023. But, even before then, initiatives such as *La Ruche qui dit Oui !* (The Beehive That Says Yes!) a French cooperative which started in 2011 and which has now spread to several francophone countries and to Spain, started helping put a stop to that. They created 'beehives' or local hubs which people could sign up to in order to buy groceries from their local producers. Not only do these beehives support small farmers and avoid the carbon footprint involved in long-distance distribution, but they also tackle both the issue of plastic wrapping and of plastic bags. Customers receive loose fruit and vegetables in crates or, at the most, in paper bags, making any use of plastic redundant.

Nevertheless, there is still a massive need to preserve food across its shelf life, and, in some cases, packaging is necessary. There are indeed some practical advantages to plastic in that respect, but nothing that innovation and research cannot tackle. This research might not actually entail reinventing the wheel but rather looking at traditional materials that have been used successfully for a long time and fixing whatever problems they present in the modern world, rather than replacing them. For example, not long ago, wax paper was commonly used to preserve food, and it is still the preferred wrapping choice for butchers and fishmongers in countries like Spain. More and more ecological shops sell reusable wax paper that can be used in combination with string or reusable elastics to cover containers such as jars. When it comes to products with a longer shelf life, such as those which are not food, eliminating the need for plastic can start at the product design stage; for example, by producing shampoo in a solid, rather than liquid, form.

Edible packages, which are made of biodegradable, plant-based materials, are also an option. They are not only turned into food for humans, but also for animals, which are primarily affected by plastic getting to the sea. For example, an innovative six-pack ring turns into turtle food by using the same ingredients as the beer contained in the cans it holds together, such as malt, barley and wheat. These edible solutions do not only avoid waste production, they also help extend shelf life. Through edible coating, vegetables like cucumbers are covered in a plant-based invisible layer which helps keep them fresher up to three times longer and which can be composted with food.

When elimination through consumption is not possible, compostable materials can offer a natural solution to waste management: for example, some companies have started making tea bags out of corn starch.

So, as we can see, innovative ideas can offer incredible solutions to tackle plastic. However, just a look at some fading traditions can already give us plenty of clues, as using plants for containing and preserving food has always been a feature of many traditional societies. For example, in some areas of Spain, the leaves of local plants are soaked and their fibres interwoven to create net bags in which fruits such as melons can be held and hung. People also use fibre string to literally sew peppers together; they then hang them off the ceiling, allowing them to dry. These peppers can even be used the year after and are still tasty and suitable for consumption.

As always with organic materials, local availability and solutions are key. For example, in some parts of the world, seaweed is a very interesting substitute material for plastic, as brown seaweed grows to up to one metre per day. Seaweed is edible and home compostable. Often, the problem with these solutions lies in cost and mass production, but the fact that companies such as the popular take-away delivery platform Just Eat have tried replacing plastic sachets in cities like London, is a promising step.

Other alternative materials derived from natural sources which are biodegradable are olive pits, sunflower hulls and even fish waste. With olive seeds, it is possible to create bioplastic granules to make packaging that can decompose in a year, as a Turkish start-up called Biolive has proven. Similarly, fish skin and scales, which would normally go to waste, can be mixed with red algae to make compostable plastic, which has been used by MarinaTex in the UK to replace single-use bags and packs.

Even those natural elements which are not edible, such as banana leaves, have long been used across the globe in areas such as Mexico, Hawaii and southeast Asia to wrap food. As well as being flexible and waterproof, they protect food from burning and keep its juices when used for cooking. Fully dried leaves are used in parts of India as packaging materials for food, and for cups. There is no danger of exploiting completely a certain type of leaf, as for example, as many as 87 plant varieties have been proven to be used for wrapping food in Turkey and the Balkans. Bamboo leaves have also been used as a wrapping material that prevents food deterioration since ancient times. In places like Malaysia and Borneo, straw mats, bamboo leaves and bamboo baskets have been used to help food stay fresh and to transport it locally. The key information is there, but, as oral traditions disappear, knowledge is distorted, wrongly leading people to believe their natural solutions are useless and leading to their abandonment.

A tradition that was also abandoned and is now being recovered is that of extracting resin from trees. Residents of rural areas in northwest Spain have, in the past decade, become resin manufacturers. Using methods which are respectful towards the pine forest, they bleed the trees to extract this powerful substance, which has historically been used to waterproof ships, light torches and treat burns, amongst other things. But arguably the biggest advantage is that this material can replace petroleum in all its uses, including plastic, with some already being made of resin at present. What also follows when local trades get revived is the chance to empower rural areas and prevent the exodus to cities, which otherwise tends to cause the ultimate destruction of these small communities.

Another organic material which is key for food preservation is earth, as was already highlighted in part I of the book. Soil enables underground storage, as well as being the core material of pottery containers. Holes have been found in the floors of Ancient Egyptian houses which would have helped to keep pots in place, and all kinds and shapes of earthen containers were used by the ancient Egyptians to preserve grain, nuts and beer, for example. As mentioned in part I, mud has the physical properties to keep the right temperature of contents, protecting them from the damaging effects of light and humidity. Since Antiquity, all the way to recent times, earthen pots have been used to preserve food, and nowadays they are still widely used in many parts of the world. In Nubia, for example, a cultural region split across the south of Egypt and north of Sudan in modern times, it is common to see large earthen vessels containing water in the streets, of a shape and manufacture for which archaeological parallels have been found in the area.

Although we cannot lose sight of the objective of moving towards more sustainable materials, it is true that, in the short term, alternative materials are unlikely to replace the vast amount of plastic we use at the moment. Therefore, another way of tackling plastic pollution right now is through improving its quality and maximising its useful life. The main goal is to make it 100% reusable, recyclable or compostable, while also guaranteeing it being free of dangerous chemicals and safe for everyone globally.

If we think about it, only a couple of decades ago, returning empty glass bottles to the shop was still common in many European countries. This enables reuse at a more global scale, though this can also happen within our own households. Refillable containers are another solution to reduce waste, though the cosmetic industry has so far been more proactive on introducing these containers for articles such as face creams and handwashes.

Ultimately, once those containers are not practical anymore, they go back into the economy through recycling or composting. The plastic can be broken down mechanically or chemically, and it can be used to make new materials. In addition, it can be composted at home or industrially.

What can I do, realistically?

So far, we have discussed proposals to reduce the amount of plastic, or to use plastic which can be easily reused or recycled. But how can we apply these principles practically when we are at home? Rather than getting frustrated about all the things you would have to change to live sustainably, it is easier to approach the task step by step and realistically, bearing in mind your personal situation and the facilities and infrastructure that surround you. To break it down in a more manageable way, we can follow the same basic three steps we have talked about above as a guide: elimination, reuse and recycling.

We cannot control whether producers, big or small, wrap their food in plastic, but we can choose to avoid buying those products that include it or that abuse its use. Of course, it depends very much on where you live. If you are in a rural area, you may be able to have easier access to local farms, but also less choice of supermarkets. In a city, there are plenty of brands to choose from, including eco-shops, but there are also less opportunities to buy directly from local producers. In general, local farmers, some of which grow organic products, tend to sell in crates, as do fresh food markets (or loose, so you can take your own fabric bags). Buying in cooperatives, like the one mentioned in the previous section, can help avoid plastic easily, while also supporting local farmers and reducing the carbon footprint incurred through transport from long distances.

If you have no alternative to buying in a supermarket, then avoiding plastic wrapping might be more difficult. But, as well as pre-packed food, they normally have sections where you can buy food off the counter, sometimes wrapped in the wax paper we mentioned above, or in other recyclable solutions, depending on the country. Some supermarkets sell, next to the groceries, reusable net bags that you can purchase to bring time and again instead of pulling one off the usual roll of plastic bags (though, more and more, such bags are also recyclable or compostable, unlike the gloves that are provided with them). These smaller reusable mesh bags can then be put into your fabric or large reusable bag. For foods like nuts and beans, traditional retailers sell by weight, and even large supermarkets have now started offering this possibility, sometimes giving you the option to bring your own container.

When it comes to other products, such as juices or milk, plastic elimination is harder. In some rural areas, it was possible until recently to practice reuse by taking large containers to farms for them to be filled up with milk. However, because the milk was not pasteurised, it had to be boiled at home to remove any possible parasites. Nowadays, this home procedure is by no means a common occurrence in most Western countries, as it is deemed unsafe.

There are still other ways in which containers can be reused. Juice or milk bottles or cartons pose more challenges, but plastic boxes with lids can be reused the way Tupperware are. In fact, some time ago it was not uncommon in countries like England to pack lunches inside cleaned margarine tubs and ice-cream containers. In general, plastic containers of the Tupperware kind can be easily replaced by glass jars, which usually have either glass or metal/plastic caps (which are not ideal, but still account for a much smaller proportion of plastic). Another obvious alternative to plastic, which we have talked about at length in the first section, is clay. Earthen containers double up as cooking pots and are extremely durable.

Both glass and clay containers can be covered with beeswax wrap, which is a great alternative to cling film and contains antibacterial properties. Cling film contains plastics or mixtures of plastic and carboard which are not as easily recyclable, while beeswax is compostable. Beeswax wraps are similar to the wax paper traditionally used by butchers and fishmongers, but many are thin enough to be activated by the warmth of your own hands, making it easier to mould them around the container. They can then be washed with cold water and mild soap and reused for about a year. Admittedly, they are not cheap, but there are also many recipes on the Internet explaining how to make wax paper yourself. With some cotton fabric, beeswax and even the pine resin previously mentioned (for extra stickiness), it is easy enough to do your own, and you can even bring them back to life by topping up the beeswax once it starts becoming less sticky.

Beyond elimination and reuse, we can focus on recycling. The only problem is that containers are often packed with lots of different bits of information and symbols that can make it completely confusing for us. Another thing to bear in mind is that local authorities have extremely different recycling policies, and what you can actually recycle and how to do it can vary enormously, so it is best to investigate first what is really feasible within your community.

We will now quickly review some of the most common symbols found on bottles, so that you can make the best decisions when buying cartons of milk or bottles of juice.

The most basic recycling symbol is a circle formed by two arrows. It means that the company has an agreement with a recycling institution so that they process their waste on their behalf. Another common symbol is a triangle formed by three arrows. Its presence does not necessarily mean the item is recyclable, but instead has a number which tells you what material it is made of, and it does not apply to plastics exclusively. Normally, the higher the number, the harder it is to recycle it. Number 1 is PET or PETE, and you will find it in a large number of bottles in the supermarket.

PET stands for polyethylene terephthalate, and, as the number indicates, is the least bad of the plastic options. Essentially, when you recycle a PET bottle, it gets cleaned and sorted by colour. Bottles that are not transparent cannot really be recycled, because the resulting product would be a dark-coloured bottle which would not work well commercially. After that sorting, PET is shredded and washed again, and it can be decontaminated further. The shreds are dried and get melted down. The resulting material, when cooled, forms pellets, which can then be used again to create other containers, like another bottle. It can also be turned into fibres, for example, for clothing. However, PET can only be recycled a limited number of times. Other containers specify whether plastic is 100% recyclable or explain where the materials come from: it is even possible to make caps for juice cartons out of sugar cane.

But not all symbols and acronyms refer to what the material is, others inform you of whether it has been sourced according to some minimum standards. FSC is a common one you can find on cartons of milk or juice, and it stands for Forest Stewardship Council, a non-profit organisation which guarantees that paper has been responsibly sourced.

By paying attention when you shop, you can avoid as much as you can those containers that do not even specify what they are made of, as well as the ones that are not as easily recyclable, such as PVC. The first time you go shopping with these considerations in mind, you will be shocked to discover the amount of plastic that it is actually used in food packaging, and you will realise the vast array of materials out there and their different degrees of recyclability.

In practice, it is very difficult to come back home from the shops with no plastic at all. So, the idea is that once you get home, you can separate your waste as best you can to maximise the recycling possibilities. Again, there is no generic rule for this. What goes into one bin in one country does not go into the same bin in another, even within Europe. The most advisable thing, as mentioned above, is for you to check what provision your local government has and how exactly recycling systems apply to your community.

This already seems an incredible setback in terms of achieving global goals when it comes to sustainability but, unfortunately, it is the current state of affairs regarding recycling. In any case, you can check the information given on the packaging itself to at least separate between organic, plastic, paper and glass at home (and even not all rubbish collection allows for organic to be thrown separately from ordinary waste). Often, public bins are colour-coded, though, again, these colours vary between countries. If you do not have containers in your street, you can make use of your local waste management plant to dispose of recyclable materials.

Ultimately, the specific reality of plastics is that it is possible to recycle all types, but this process poses a lot of logistical difficulties, and it can be too costly to be considered worth it. Some plastics are too small to be recycled, and others cannot be recycled unless labels are separated and there are no residues in the container, so cleanliness is also a factor. This is the reason why recycling is considered a last step, and elimination and reuse are preferred options when it comes to minimising plastic use.

While all these considerations are important to build a sustainable future, the truth is that there is already an enormous build-up of plastic in our seas which cannot be eliminated unless we do something about it. This was the aim of the Ocean Cleanup Project, which, incredibly, was originally devised by an eighteen-year-old. After various prototypes, the project is now a reality which attracts millions of dollars in funding; the last haul managed to bring back a whopping 9,000 kilograms of plastic. This waste can then be recycled and used to build new products, such as sunglasses, whose sale also helps fund the project. The Ocean Clean Project installation consists of an artificial floating coastline that gathers plastic towards itself as if it was an enormous arm, with the waste then going into a funnel-shaped net. This device is towed by two boats, and it takes advantage of the natural current to help bring the rubbish into the net. Of course, there are still disadvantages to this, such as the use of fuel, but Dutch entrepreneur Boyan Slat is constantly looking at ways to improve the system. For now, this technique only works to collect surface plastic and does not tackle the massive problem of sunken plastics and microplastics, but it is a tremendous step towards eliminating plastic out of our oceans.

Chapter 3: Building a future

As we have seen in the previous section, the food production industry is one of the most polluting sectors in the world. Another industry that contributes largely to air pollution and waste generation, as well as energy usage, is the construction sector.

The construction industry is very susceptible to being abused. Needless to say, shelter is a basic human right, and the growing global demand has highly unjust dynamics as a consequence. The need to build fast and in large quantities means that often the cheapest and fastest materials to produce prevail. Despite steps being taken towards establishing energy efficiency ratings, the main focus is not on producing buildings which are suitable for their surroundings, but rather on meeting the demand for housing in often already overcrowded cities.

In contrast, building materials, ventilation, light and orientation are important housing considerations which cultures have paid attention to since ancient times. Just like many other pieces of knowledge on how to make the most of our surroundings, information about the ways to build shelter was passed on from generation to generation. Although this would have happened at domestic level, it is precisely that wealth of knowledge related to traditional architecture that has deteriorated the most. Historically, official and religious buildings have perhaps had more luck. They have been better protected from destruction, which means architects have been able to observe the ancient application of principles such as light and air circulation.

Tourism is a double-edge sword when it comes to this preservation: while in some parts of the world traditional architecture has been wildly destroyed, in others, dwellings have turned into a tourist attraction. In Qurna, in Upper Egypt, traditional Egyptian mudbrick houses were systematically destroyed throughout the years because they were seen as 'visual pollution' for tourists visiting the famous ancient Egyptian temples of Luxor and Karnak. In contrast, traditional thatched cottages attract tourists to regions such as the Cotswolds, in the south of England.

Sadly, when it comes to domestic architecture, the replacement of traditional materials (such as earth) for mass-produced ones (such as red brick and concrete) has been a big blow for sustainability. Traditional materials are sourced locally, which means that transport costs are eliminated or reduced dramatically, consequently decreasing pollution. These materials are also naturally suited to the surroundings, so they can help create the right temperature and humidity conditions for local buildings. The problem is that they are only useful if people know how to employ them properly and, when that oral knowledge is not preserved, traditional architecture disappears just as any other craft would do.

Ultimately, not just the use, but also the reuse of local building materials has been a constant throughout history since ancient times, as they were considered valuable and practical elements. If you visit, for example, any of the medieval English cathedrals close to Hadrian's Wall, which acted as the border of the Roman Empire for several hundred years at the beginning of the Christian era, you will be able to spot reused blocks belonging to this large construction. The examples are endless and can be found across the world. Even nowadays, if you walk around Egyptian villages, it is not uncommon to find slabs from ancient temples that have been repurposed as house door thresholds, for example.

Regulations mean that houses are barely built by owners anymore in many countries, and perceptions of what is suitable are highly influenced by a sense of what is respectable and modern – and for a large part of the developing world that means 'Western' styles. A vicious circle concerning the quality of traditional domestic architecture is created: the less traditional houses are built, the less people know how to build them and the worse their perception is of them, partially because they are not being used correctly, which results in uncomfortable domestic environments. That is why projects that document traditional crafts, be it architecture, basketry or pottery, are so essential.

If we want buildings to be a key part of a sustainable future, we must work to preserve past practices and learn from millennia of locally developed solutions. As well as the use of local materials, these solutions refer to ventilation, orientation and light strategies. At a time when energy prices are soaring, they can not only provide global solutions and be enhanced by modern technology, but they can also be a source of relevant ideas that we can implement as individuals to different degrees.

Ventilation is an essential consideration, particularly as increasing desertification means higher temperatures for large areas of the globe. Devices such as air-conditioning units are costly and consume large amounts of electricity. As well as being out of reach for many, they are not a sustainable solution. Before these were available, builders in harsh climates adopted solutions such as the wind catcher. This was an architectural device already known to the ancient Egyptians, as shown in the tomb of an official called Nebamun, dated to 1300 BCE. Wind catchers were brick-vaulted or wickerwork wind scoops, which faced north and were angled downwards, to capture the cool wind of the north and channel it into the rooms. They were placed on the terrace, having a triangular aspect when viewed from the side. Paired with a plan orientation to the north, they helped cool the house.

A similar device was the wind chimney, traditionally made of dense materials such as stone and mud that absorbed the heat from the air as it moved down the chimney and had cooled it by the time it came out from the bottom.

A traditional component of Mediterranean architecture, the central courtyard, also responds to this requirement. If you have ever been to a traditional patio house in southern Spain, you would have noticed that they usually have water devices and plenty of greenery. These all allow cross-ventilation, making cool air available during the day and protecting interiors from it at night. One of the most beautiful buildings in the world, La Alhambra of Granada, in Andalusia, is a prime example of this technique to create a pleasant and cool environment that has served as a refuge from the intense summer heat for centuries.

Another great device traditionally used to control internal temperature are wooden shutters, which prevent sunlight from entering the house in the hottest moments of the day, while allowing the breeze to enter through their slits.

The openings themselves can be adapted to specific wind conditions and local geography to maximise cross-ventilation or to prevent the effects of the prevailing weather in the area. Plan orientation can similarly help in this regard. For example, in countries with coastal areas which were badly exposed to wind and sea fret, front doors were traditionally positioned at the back of the house to protect from the elements.

If you have ever wondered why walls in Greek villages, for example, are completely painted white, light is the answer. White walls reflect the sun, so the house does not absorb the heat. Similarly, the blue colours so closely identified with places such as Santorini, also contribute to keeping spaces cool.

Again, through the positioning of the windows, the amount of natural light can be maximised according to the time of the year. Moorish architecture, as well as being a great example of natural ventilation, mastered light through the use of sky lights, which allowed light to penetrate deeply into the building. Light management can also be applied to the position of rooms in some cultures, with bedrooms facing east to make the most of the morning light and spaces such as bathrooms and storerooms in darker areas. In other cultures, however, the activities would have been moved around the house to adapt to the available light at different times of the day, rather than having designated rooms with a fixed function.

Documenting traditional ways of building and promoting and applying their principles as much as possible are key aspects of tackling climate change. Some human groups that have adapted to life in harsh conditions, such as extreme flooding, have developed techniques to make this environment work for them. This has been the case for thousands of years in the southern wetlands of Iraq, where the Ma'dan have built floating villages. They make use of a species of reed, called Qasab, that grows naturally in that environment to build islands over water. These skilled traditional builders can raise their arched structures, completely built out of bundled reeds secured with rope, which is also made from the same material, in only three days. The dried reed can be used for walls, but also for floors and roofs, and the structures can last beyond 25 years.

This reed is a fundamental part of their lives, as it also serves as food for water buffalos and is used to make flour.

Water is, of course, an essential part of life, and communities near springs have made the most of that natural resource. Harie, in Japan, is such a community. All houses have an adjacent kind of shed built on top of water, and the liquid naturally flows up sinks where vegetables can be washed. Fish actually live in that clean water and are considered part of the household, feeding on vegetable scraps. The water flow is kept pure through a circular system, and the neighbours make sure not to use any polluting soaps inside their houses. The water then flows into a lake which is home to an ecosystem of thousands of plant and fish species. As well as providing an incredibly eco-friendly environment, this efficient way of making use of natural resources also creates community ties. Those who are downstream rely on those who live upstream to make sure that water remains pure and safe to use.

Another way of dealing with flooding can be found in Benin, West Africa. There, the Tofinu tribe built stilted houses around a canal system that can be navigated by canoe. The buildings include everything the community might need, such as a bank, a post office, a mosque, etc. The lake city is surrounded by 12,000 fish paddocks that feed the people that live there and, despite being made by humans, do not need any chemicals and increase biodiversity, in the same manner as mangrove ecosystems naturally do.

Sadly, mangroves elsewhere, such as in India or the Philippines are disappearing, invaded by plastic waste. These important ecosystems, which provide coastal communities with a protection from flooding, can only be restored by projects that plant trees at a large scale.

Reforestation is also key to recovering forests after illegal gold mining poisons the water and the soil. Efforts made in Colombia, for example, combine the planting of trees with beekeeping to create new financial resources.

The same fishponds technique as that of Benin is actually used in Calcutta, a place with a massive water pollution problem caused in no small part by the clothing industry, as we will see in the Dressed for Success section below, but also by sewage. On the outskirts though, an indigenous technology of 300 fishponds cleans the water and produces food. Incredibly, just as it happens in many other cases, many countries around the world are seeking this technology, while in Calcutta itself, where it is already present, it is threatened by development. The symbiosis of algae and bacteria, the sunshine and its effect on the sewage clears wastewater in around a month.

As described, organic resources can offer effective solutions to sustainability problems, and elimination of polluting alternatives, as we have seen for food production and consumption, would be the ideal option. Again, this is simply not feasible in many cases, so reuse and recycling are the next steps to bear in mind.

In terms of using organic materials, modern technology can help overcome the difficulties and enhance their properties. For example, 'hempcrete' blocks are blocks made of hemp and lime, which promote affordable and healthier housing. These blocks are fire resistant, light and perform well thermally. In addition, they have a low environmental impact, as their carbon footprint is small. Not only that, but hemp is also a good substitute for plastic: the cellulose of the stalk has been used to produce cellophane and rayon. Hemp is also used to make 'hempwool', an insulation material which is organic, healthy and toxin free.

Reuse and recycle are possible even with less desirable materials, such as plastic. Nzambi Matee, a Kenyan engineer, was tired of seeing plastic invading her community and not being properly disposed of, and she also wanted to come up with some durable housing solutions. In order to achieve that, she decided to make bricks out of plastic. She created a system which converts high density polyethylene, low density polyethylene, and polypropylene plastics into solid bricks through shredding them and mixing them with sand. These bricks are actually affordable and more resistant than concrete.

Similarly, ReWall is a board material made 100% from the entire composite materials of the cartons used in drink containers which otherwise would end up in landfills, and that can be purposed as exterior sheathing, wallboard, and floor underlayment.

Luckily, as well as these innovations pushed by individuals, there are organisations such as INTBAU which aim to initiate programmes that respond to local contexts, and that promote the essential role of tradition in the built environment. Divided aptly in national chapters, INTBAU maintain several journals, organise workshops, exhibitions and competitions to encourage the preservation of traditional building techniques and the knowledge related to local architectures. They also recognise and promote the work of traditional artisans, many of which come from a long family tradition. In doing so, they help keep traditional building trades and techniques alive, and promote a more sustainable way of building for future communities across the world.

The challenge for the future is to combine solutions for the three aspects we have mentioned so far – food production and consumption, waste management and building – to create a new type of community.

Following the Paris Agreement, the European Union developed the European Green Pact, with the idea of helping Europe grow in a more sustainable way. One of the most important parts of the pact is the Farm to Fork initiative, which aims to create circular communities, where architecture and food production are focused on being self-sufficient.

The COVID crisis has done nothing but increase the need for the kind of community based on local food and energy production, and remote work. The more that can be made out of nearby resources the better, empowering neighbourhoods.

Cities must be reinvented in the future to face climate change challenges and bring together environment, infrastructures, housing, urbanism and information technology to create an energy efficient and self-sufficient community. If we are to look at current proposals, there is a strong chance that trees and plants, even entire mini forests on top of buildings, will play a key part.

Teams from different countries have tried to come up with designs that develop these concepts. For example, in

Copenhagen, a design team researched the viability of creating a 'port farm', where seafood could be bred in a sustainable manner, and then be directly used for consumption locally. The project included mussel farms on top of which restaurants and other facilities were placed, and through the use of geothermal energy and a natural waste management system, a sustainable project was devised. Also in Denmark, a development project has been planned for an area with sustainable houses and reforestation, with a circular economy in mind. They combine good planting techniques with a rich soil, first planting trees and then reducing these to plant vegetation sublayers which increase biodiversity. In the forest, edible cultivation is prioritised, so that it becomes a key part of the community that can both be used recreationally and to obtain food. By sharing outdoor areas and optimising infrastructures, it is possible to have the same living density as in the traditional neighbourhoods, but sustainably.

In addition, the building materials are natural, recyclable and energy efficient, saving money, energy and CO_2 emissions, and several types of houses and property models are included to make the community more varied.

The idea is also to share services the community can feel a part of and that cater for different members, such as creche, canteen, coworking, and health services. In addition, urban farms guarantee deliveries of weekly fresh and organic products to the neighbours, supporting local farmers and improving the food production and consumption processes.

The aim of these projects is therefore to link people to communities, and these communities to nature, in this way tackling the many industry, sustainability and housing challenges that we face in the 21st century.

The hope is that authorities will get on board and that this type of urbanisation will become the norm in the future. Amongst the challenges ahead, there are: the fact that the housing industry moves so much money in some countries, that an investment is needed the benefits of which might not be seen straightaway, and that other powerful industries with different motivations, such as the banking sector, often play a big part in decisions over housing developments.

Ultimately, the built spaces proposed for the future are based on rebuilding lost local networks of trades and production, synergies and the sense of belonging and mutual cooperation that characterised the fabric of local communities, examples of which can be found across time and space. Again, looking back in our own history and gaining an awareness of current existing practices, such as those of the Harie community, are essential parts of any future developments.

What can I do, realistically?

The luxury of being able to build your own house from scratch with the help of an architect to assist you in making it as sustainable as possible in every respect is accessible to very few people. Even solar panels, despite their obvious benefits, particularly in countries with many days of sunshine, such as Spain, require an investment that is not within everyone's reach. Admittedly, it is often difficult and expensive to retrofit some of these innovations, particularly in flats. However, the aim of this book is both to make you aware of innovations at a global level and to suggest realistic ways in which organic materials can help you achieve a more sustainable way of living.

If you live in a house, placing trees and water features in yards is an option which will help you regulate the temperature (even in the balcony of a flat, plants help to do this). Deciduous trees can cast a shadow in summer, protecting the façade from the heat, while in the winter, the lack of leaves allows for the warmth of the sun to bathe the house without interference. Organic fabric can also help you shade the façade through the use of a sail or canopy.

Conversely, fabric can help you keep the house warm indoors. If you use heavy curtains and draw them as soon as the sun goes down in the winter, you will reduce the amount of cold and draught coming into the house. Similarly, draught excluders placed at the bottom of doors prevent heat from escaping the house and thus will help with your gas or electricity bills.

Wooden shutters also help regulate light and air coming into the house, whilst fabric blinds help add warmth and minimise draughts. Insulation is also essential for energy efficiency and, as mentioned, there are several organic alternatives, though they can be hard to retrofit in a flat, and they also make spaces smaller as they require the gap within walls to be wider.

Hanging decorative fabric on the walls can also help keep rooms warm, as does using natural fibre rugs.

In summary, even if you are not able to build your house in the most sustainable way or even to retrofit the latest innovations to make it healthier and more energy-efficient, there is a range of things you can do to live in a more organic way and do your bit for the environment, which in turn will also save you money.

Chapter 4: Dressed for success

As we have seen, together with shelter and food, clothing is one of human's basic needs. Since the beginning of human history, our ancestors used animal skin to protect their bodies from the elements, later turning them into more complex clothing by sewing different parts together, and then, after the last ice age, favouring textiles and creating woven garments with plant fibres.

Researchers such as Ian Gilligan say that there is evidence that our early ancestors saw clothes mainly as a way of coping with extremely cold temperatures and were happy enough to walk around in the nude when the temperature was warmer. This is backed up by contemporary human groups, such as the Tasmanians in Australia, which until colonisation saw no need for clothing if the temperature did not require it. In both cases, ancient and modern, other means of social expression and community identification were available to them, such as tattoos, body paint and scarification (skin incisions). Throughout time, though, clothes evolved and became much more linked to social and cultural rules.

At some point in history, perhaps because of clothes becoming more extensively needed through the year, a sense of embarrassment was developed at being naked in front of others. Later on, of course, moral and religious considerations would take over in demanding people were clothed at all times in public. It is such an obvious requirement for most societies nowadays, that we almost find it hard to imagine it could have ever been any different.

Although, just as our ancestors did, we can convey our identity through other means, and many people do use clothing to express their personality. Others might think they do not give it any importance, but, to one extent or another, we all express ourselves through what we wear. Some people will only wear black or white, and many choose more or less colourful clothes depending on mood and time of the year (and summer is always a winner when it comes to bright, happy colours). Colour is deeply embedded in our cultural traditions, which is why it often has such a symbolic role in certain important moments for the life of an individual and their community. For example, white is associated with marriage in some parts of the world, while red performs this role in some other cultures. Many Western cultures think of black as the colour of mourning, while in others death is thought of as a rebirth, and white conveys renewal and purity. In short, colour has been extensively used since ancient history to make a statement, whether about personal choices, place within the community or social class, or to mark certain events in the life of an individual.

These different colour garments are achieved through the use of dyes. For a large part of history, these dyes were natural and extracted from plants, insects or molluscs. The evidence for the use of natural dyes probably goes back as far as 10,200 BCE and extends until the middle of the 19th century, when synthetic dyes were developed. Amongst the most popular and most ancient dyes was indigo, a blue colour derived from the leaves of the woad herb and the indigo plant. Some other colours, such as red and yellow, were also derived from plants. Other red shades came from scale insects. A plant still used today to dye leather and silk is the logwood, which yields a substance that, once oxidised, turns from red to charcoal and grey and is nowadays mixed with the chemical chromium to produce black.

Other colours, such as purple, became so exclusive because they were hard to extract. Tyrian purple was extracted from the glands of snails, so you can imagine how many little molluscs had to be killed for just a dash of colour. Because it was so hard to obtain this colour, purple garments were deemed exclusive and were only meant for upper class individuals such as Roman magistrates, emperors, and, later in history, for top members of the Catholic church hierarchy.

As many other industries did, the textile industry grew during the Industrial Revolution, leading to the development of synthetic alternatives to dyes. A turning point was the discovery of mauve, the first synthetic dye. Coal tar was then used to develop more than 50 different compounds with this purpose and from then onwards the dyeing industry did nothing but increase.

What most of us do not have in mind when choosing colourful clothing, is that dyeing fabrics to produce different colours is the part of the clothes-making process that requires the most water. Not only that, but the clothing industry as a whole is, according to many reports, the second industry after food production that consumes the most water in the world. Some popular crops, such as cotton, are particularly demanding when it comes to water. But water usage is not the worst part of it, as dye wastewater is often poured into the rivers without any prior treatment, ending up in the sea and heavily polluting water sources.

Another way in which clothes contribute to pollution and health hazards is through the pesticides used to cultivate the crops fabrics are made of. Both these pesticides and synthetic dyes can cause health issues such as skin rashes.

The main way of avoiding these hazards is through the use of organic textiles, which can have both a positive environmental and social impact. Organic textiles are those grown without the use of chemical fertilisers and pesticides, and which do not rely on genetically modified seeds. Weeds are removed manually, and natural pesticides and fertilizers are used. By avoiding chemical fertilisers, rivers are also protected.

The advantages for the environment are obvious: by using alternatives to fossil-fuel fertilisers, soils remain healthier and are able to store carbon, which in turn contributes to fighting climate change. In addition, these soils are capable of absorbing water in times of flooding and to retain it when the weather is dry. For example, the Soil Association, based in the UK, includes in its website technical resources and knowledge to help farmers achieve better soils. They also provide a guarantee, the Global Organic Textiles Standard logo, that certifies that natural techniques and products have been used.

Organic cotton production, for example, can also be combined with other crops, which helps keeps soils healthy and in turn also provides a more stable source of food for farmers and their communities.

Just as we saw for architecture, mixing traditional practices with the latest innovation can prove essential in achieving sustainable solutions for the future and counteract the effects of fast fashion. An example of this is an incredibly resourceful engineer,

Veena Sahajwalla, who has devised a way of turning old, discarded clothes into tiles. Inspired by her upbringing in Mumbai, where nothing goes to waste, she has come up with different ways of repurposing waste in Australia, where she now lives. By mixing old clothes with bits of glass, also previously disposed of by people, she has been able to produce a range of tiles that can be used for kitchens, bathrooms and general decoration. Not only that, but, through her inventions, she is also enabling waste collectors, such as those that gather mattresses, to process the different parts to manufacture tiles locally and independently, enabling them to have a source of revenue to support their activities.

What can I do, realistically?

There are plenty of ways in which you can help reduce the environmental cost of clothing, but admittedly, they are not always the cheapest option. Organic garments tend to have higher prices than their ordinary alternatives. However, their benefits are not just environmental but also personal, particularly for people with sensitive skin and/or children. Another thing worth bearing in mind is that the fast fashion system whereby constant new collections are produced to fit consumer whims just for a season is not sustainable in any way, environmentally or humanly. Neither is the mass production of clothes sold for ridiculously cheap prices.

As always, the first option is to eliminate, but since clothes are not something we can do without nowadays (although, in many cases, we could do with a lot less items than we own), organic textiles that eliminate harmful chemicals and encourage healthy soils are preferrable. As was explained in part I of this book, we must distinguish between organically grown textiles such as those described above, and organic material sources in general. For example, leather is organic in the definition used throughout this book, as it comes from animals. However, it is traditionally treated with harmful chemicals and in that sense, it is not an organically produced material.

In fact, some people refuse to use leather for ethical reasons. As was previously remarked, vegans and some vegetarians are against its use because of its animal origin. Others think of it as a by-product of breeding livestock rather than an end, and do not have a problem with using it. A more objective fact is that tanneries, the places where leather is processed, have many negative environmental effects due to their high energy and water usage and due to the chemicals involved in the treatment of the material. Some progress has been made towards controlling these steps though, such as the creation of the Leather Working Group, which keeps an eye on the supply chain and provides feedback to manufacturers.

The biggest obstacle to replace leather is that many of the alternatives are plastic-based, generate microplastics and are therefore a worse problem than the potential one they are trying to solve. As we have seen, microplastics are a real and objective problem both for humans and for sea animals, which mistake them for food. A more suitable alternative, rather than reinventing the material, is replacing the chemicals used in its treatment by natural vegetable tannins, which are organic and biodegradable.

The environmental hazards of clothes dyeing also apply to jeans, and not only because of the chemicals used in the process, but also because of the large amounts of water required to wash and bleach jeans. Certain brands of jeans have attempted to use new technology to avoid this massive waste, for example, by using laser to bleach trousers. Unfortunately, these options still come at a less than affordable price and are by no means within everyone's reach.

Another option is to do your best to avoid certain materials which are particularly harmful, such as polyester. Polyester manufacturing uses harmful chemicals, which can contribute to water pollution if not disposed of properly. Just like plastic alternatives to leather, polyester sheds millions of plastic microfibres when washed.

There are alternatives to these textiles, such as hemp, lyocell or bamboo. Lyocell features more and more in high street garments. It is a cellulose made from wood, usually eucalyptus, which does not require large amounts of watering or pesticides. However, it has the disadvantage of needing a lot of energy. Equally, hemp uses less water, but also requires a lot of energy. If they are to be true sustainable alternatives, this energy would also need to be produced in sustainable ways.

The first step is, therefore, to bring the minimum amount of highly polluting fabrics into your house.

As always, after elimination, the second sustainable principle is reuse. There are plenty of shops that sell them and, in recent years, mobile apps to sell second-hand clothes have also proliferated. Of course, plenty of children and adults have traditionally reused clothes within their immediate or extended family and continue to do so.

Those who are handier even convert clothes into different ones to give them a new use. There are plenty of YouTube channels where you can find ideas on how to turn your garments into new ones, or even into different objects, such as wall organisers and cotton bags. In the No Time to Waste section, we also talked about manufacturing your own beeswax food wraps using pieces of fabric as a surface to extend the beeswax mixture on. Needless to say, old clothes can also be repurposed for kitchen and dust cloths.

There are also certain companies which encompass both reuse and recycling of clothes, with a social focus. You can both donate your clothes and buy second-hand clothes in their shops. They then invest part of this money into social projects. The idea is to give a second life to the clothes that you do not use anymore. There are plenty of containers where you can leave your used clothes and these are then collected and either sold in the shops if they are in a good enough condition, sold to local sellers in other countries, or recycled. While this model allows for big volumes of clothes to be managed, it is sometimes criticised for its bureaucracy and business operation, with some saying that not enough of a percentage ends up being used charitably and that the clothes processing is more of a business and a tax fiddling device for the benefit of a few organisations than anything else.

Research well what company you go for and evaluate the pros and cons, and whether their numbers add up for you. If you decide that you are not comfortable with the business side of things, there are always other charitable organisations which redistribute clothes locally rather than trading with them.

Closing the organic cycle

For a long time, the three Rs of sustainability were reduce, reuse and recycle. Throughout this second part of the book, we have focused on ways in which these three principles (or elimination, rather than reduction) can be applied to food production and consumption, waste management, architecture and the clothing industry.

Nowadays, up to 7 principles are proposed and, although with some variations, they generally complete the three original principles by adding: redesign, renovate, repair and recover. Some of these principles overlap and have been hinted at throughout the various sections.

Redesign is about thinking of products from the design stage in a way that makes them last longer and that does not create as much waste or creates waste which can then be recycled. Biodegradable products, such as the beer packs made of edible algae, are great examples of redesigned packaging.

Repairing an object is a logical choice and one that has been consistently used throughout history until recent times, as we can tell from the archaeological record. Absurdly, fast fashion and mass production, and the disappearance of skilled workers in the repairing sector, have meant that repairing things such as electrical appliances usually work out more expensive than buying new ones. Often, companies purposely avoid making parts available for repair to prompt customers to buy new devices, in a process that has been dubbed 'technical obsolescence' and that has generated shocking amounts of difficult to manage waste in recent decades.

Of course, regardless of this Western trend, many groups across the world have continued to repair objects, saving energy and avoiding unnecessary waste, and the act is even an important traditional part of some cultures. *Kintsugi*, as the art of repairing is called in Japanese culture, also transcends the practical purposes of objects and has a philosophical justification. By repairing pottery with gold or silver lacquer, the breaks are highlighted rather than hidden, but this is considered to make the object all the more beautiful. This tradition, which has existed for centuries, places the emphasis on the history of the object and appreciates it for what makes it unique.

Another one of the seven principles is renovating. Renovating is, in reality, very similar to repairing, only that the original object does not need to be broken. Instead, the old object is updated to create, for example, a vintage piece of furniture or a garment.

The last of the principles is recovering. Recovering consists of retrieving products that are going to be thrown and using them with other aims or repurposing them. Recovering can lead to innovations such as the tile making explained in the Dressed for Success section, which manufactured new products through the recycling of clothes and glass that had been thrown out.

Often, our cultural bias prevents us from thinking of ways in which we could recycle, but we must remember that animal excrements have been a fundamental part of cultivation through history, with dung being used as fuel since the Neolithic period. In addition, since the 17th century, we have been able to obtain flammable gas from decaying organic matter. And if animal faeces can be made useful in that way, why not human waste? Actually, many developing countries do have private anaerobic digesters, and in the West, there has been larger plants that produce heat and electricity from both animal and human waste.

A British inventor, Brian Harper, has taken the strengths of excrements further. He has devised a way of powering streetlamps with them. In an anaerobic digester, microorganisms turn the dog poo deposited by owners as they take their pets for a walk into methane, which powers light. Ten bags can power light for around two hours.

Faeces are also being repurposed in Ontario, Canada, where they have devised a system to collect excrements in parks, which are then taken by trucks to a plant where they are turned into methane and then into electricity.

Both at a small and a large scale, biodigesters can play a great role in this. They are a common feature in some developing countries, where they are used to create methane gas from cow manure to be used as fuel. A social initiative in India has used this to power a groundwater pump. The resulting water is then filtered and bottled and sold for a cheap price that contributes to funding the expenses. The idea is closely connected to improving sanitation.

These anaerobic digesters have been used at a larger scale to generate biomethane to be injected into the grid, in order to provide fuel to between 5,000 and 6,000 homes. While this has the inconvenience of the transport involved in moving the waste to a plant, an alternative solution exists: automated modules which act as anaerobic digesters and can be installed in shipping containers, which can be used locally by individuals.

These individual solutions have also been supported by governments such as that of the Netherlands, who have helped farmers install anaerobic digesters that collect cow dung and transform it into biogas. There are also other machines that extract nitrate and phosphate for fertiliser that can be operated simultaneously. The scheme works through leasing, and farmers then obtain a fixed 12-year price for the biogas produced. In 20 days, farms can produce enough fuel to power three homes for a year.

Another field that has benefited from the use of sewage has been transport. Also in the UK, a bus powered by gas generated from sewage and food waste can go for 300 km on a full tank.

But excrement has not only become useful for energy and transport, it has also been considered for the building industry, and even to feed animals. Attempts to produce carbon-neutral bricks through the combination of incinerating sewage and ash have been made. Again, storing dung patties on top of rooves to be used for fuel is a common sight in traditional mudbrick houses in Egypt.

Also, faeces have been used to feed the larvae of a type of insect, called black soldier fly, which are then eaten by chickens or fish.

But human waste also refers, of course, to urine, which can have many purposes too. In the same way as biologists have used yeast for years to create vaccines, yeast could be fed with nutrients from urine to produce other drugs.

But, without thinking so hypothetically, urine can be as useful as faeces when it comes to generating electricity, as has been proven by microbial fuel cells powered by urine and solar-powered urinals that generate hydrogen fuel. Although the fact that this technique was tried out at the famous Glastonbury music festival might sound peculiar, the technology can be ground-breaking for emergency areas and refugee camps.

Funnily enough, urine is already being used in outer space to provide clean drinking water for American astronauts in the International Space Station. The expectations are that, in the future, astronauts will self-sufficiently produce the nutrients and materials they need through using their own urine to feed yeast often found in cheese. This would really help the mission by providing materials *in situ*, rather than having to bring them from Earth, as well as saving lots of space and making the trip more comfortable.

Scientists even go as far as thinking that the CO_2 exhaled by astronauts could help photosynthetic organisms, such as algae, to produce carbon-based substances. These algae could then also be used to feed the yeast, the same as urine.

As well as feeding astronauts, the yeast could even be used in the future to make the plastic used in 3D printers, that in turn could be used to produce all sorts of items while out in space. Even faeces could be involved again to create organic material to help support the yeast growth, though more investigation is required.

With missions often being criticised for polluting space with lots of waste, and since the space race is unlikely to slow down in the near future, exploring the possibilities of making astronauts' lives more self-sufficient seems a positive development, and the source of raw materials is, of course, endless.

Conclusion

The idea for this book stemmed from my love of organic things, and my amazement at how they could be preserved so well for thousands of years. I always found that organic objects, such as a papyrus pair of sandals, or a piece of linen, brought us a lot closer to our ancestors than golden masks or lavishly decorated chests ever could.

It also came from the frustration of seeing traditional trades in different fields disappear unrecorded across the world in the name of a badly understood modernity, while answers were sought for the very problems that those traditional solutions were trying to tackle.

I have given but a few brushstrokes on how humans have made use of by-products of earth, plants and animals to adapt to the environment and to develop their creativity and their artistic endeavours. We have also looked at how these products are still a massive part of both the everyday and the beliefs of current human groups across the world.

The task of repairing the link between old knowledge and new challenges was an ambitious one, and this book has only very humbly addressed it. But I do hope it has given you food for thought, and an interest in investigating and preserving old lore. I also hope it has made you feel more connected to our ancestors in a global way, as well as giving you ideas on how to live your life more sustainably and make the most of your surroundings in a way which respects nature.

If we are to repair the damage done to the planet, particularly since the Industrial Revolution, and to build a fairer and more sustainable world, innovation and research will be key. But this must be paired with the recognition, preservation and recording of traditional techniques for food production, building, nature adaptation and general everyday practices.

Political and bureaucracy issues give a grim perspective in what concerns the future of the planet, as has recently been seen in the Cop26, in Glasgow, where countries were unable to reach agreements about the cuts in polluting emissions over the coming years. Of course, big corporations also have an enormous influence over political decisions.

However, the younger generations seem determined to push for more sustainable living. They are much more aware of the facts, they have the tools to access the information and to share it. Wherever the issues are being discussed, they are ready to put up a fight, and that is very promising. If we can also interest them in the past and the wealth of knowledge that it brings, we will be arming them with the necessary tools to create a sustainable future. There are also many people across the world, from engineers to consumers, who are genuinely worried about the state of things and want them to improve by acting before it is too late. Their innovations, creativity, enthusiasm and thirst for knowledge offer some hope. Hopefully, this book has contributed to supporting their – and our – fight.

References

Part I: Birth

Chapter 1

- Boric, D. (2008): "First Households And 'House Societies' In European Prehistory. Prehistoric Europe". *Theory and Practice.* 109-142

- Bryan, C. P. (1930): Ancient Egyptian Medicine. The Papyrus Ebers. Ares, Chicago.

- Budka, J. "Egyptian Impact on Pot-Breaking Ceremonies at El-Kurru? A Re-Examination", in Julie R. Anderson, Derek W. Welsby (eds.), *The fourth cataract and beyond. Proceedings of the 12th International Conference for Nubian Studies*, 2014, 641-654

- Ceramic Arts Network (2021): www.ceramicartsnetwork.org

- Claystation (2021): www.claystation.com

- Cooney, K. (2010): "Gender Transformation in Death: A Case Study of Coffins from Ramesside Period Egypt". *Near Eastern Archaeology* 73:4 (2010), 224-237

- Duram, L. (2019): "Organic food". https://www.britannica.com/topic/organic-food

- Frink, L. and Karen G. "The Beauty of "Ugly" Eskimo Cooking Pots", American Antiquity, Jan., 2008, Vol. 73, No. 1, 103-120

- Hsieh, J. "The Practice of Repairing Vessels in Ancient Egypt: Methods of Repair and Anthropological Implications", *Near Eastern Archaeology*, Vol. 79, No. 4 (December 2016), 280-283

- Kaimal, G, Ray, K. & Muniz, J. "Reduction of Cortisol Levels and Participants' Responses Following Art Making", *Art Therapy*, (2016). 33:2, 74-80

- Simpson, C. (2001): "Mud things in Qurna". http://qurna.org/article6.htm

- Singer, C. (1965): *A history of technology*, Oxford University Press, Oxford.

- Schiaparelli, E. (2007): *La tomba intatta dell'architetto Kha nella Necropli di Tebe, Torino, Relazione sui lavori della Missione archeologica Italiana in Egitto (1903-1920)* II. AdArte.

- Stevanovic, M. "The Age of Clay: The Social Dynamics of House Destruction", *Journal Of Anthropological Archaeology* 16, 334–395 (1997)

- The Pottery Experience (2021): https://www.thepotteryexperience.co.uk/making

- Wenzel Geissler, P. "The Significance of Earth-Eating: Social and Cultural Aspects of Geophagy among Luo Children", *Journal of the International African Institute*, Vol. 70, No. 4 (2000), 653-682

- World Housing Encyclopedia. A joint project by EERI and IAEE (www.world-housing.net). "Major construction types".

Chapter 2

- Aranguren, B. et al. "Early Neanderthal Wooden Artifacts from Italy". *Proceedings of the National Academy of Sciences,* Feb 2018, 115 (9) 2054-2059

- Crop Trust (2021): "Svalbard Global Seed Vault". https://www.croptrust.org/our-work/svalbard-global-seed-vault/

- Child, F. J. (2015): *The English and Scottish Popular Ballads, 1*. Cambridge University Press. Cambridge.

- Dehghan, S. K. (2019): "Are Mexican avocados the world's new conflict commodity?". *The Guardian*. https://www.theguardian.com/global-development/2019/dec/30/are-mexican-avocados-the-worlds-new-conflict-commodity

- Giles, S. (2018): "Ancient Egyptian Parents Put This In Their Child's Grave To Play With In The Afterlife". *Museum Crush*. https://museumcrush.org/ancient-egyptian-parents-put-this-in-their-childs-grave-to-play-with-in-the-afterlife/

- Gilligan, I. (2018): *Climate, Clothing, and Agriculture in Prehistory: Linking Evidence, Causes, and Effects*. Cambridge University Press.

- Greenwell, M., & Rahman, P. K. (2015): "Medicinal Plants: Their Use in Anticancer Treatment". *International Journal of Pharmaceutical Sciences and Research*, 6(10), 4103–4112.

- Lobel, J. A. (2016): "Dressing for the Ages". *Archaeology*. 69 (3), 9.

- Meskell, L. (2002): *Private life in New Kingdom Egypt*. Princeton University Press. Princeton, Oxford.

- Morris, C. A. (2017): "A Tale of Fish from Two Countries". *U.S. Department of Agriculture*. https://www.usda.gov/media/blog/2016/12/05/tale-fish-two-countries

- Smithsonian National Museum of Natural History. (2021): "What does it mean to be human?" https://humanorigins.si.edu/human-characteristics/tools-food

- Spinazzi-Lucchesi, C. (2018): *The Unwound Yarn Birth and Development of Textile Tools Between Levant and Egypt.* Edizioni Ca'Foscari. Venezia.

- Willcox, D. *et al.* (2009): "The Okinawan Diet: Health Implications of a Low-Calorie, Nutrient-Dense, Antioxidant-Rich Dietary Pattern Low in Glycemic Load". *Journal of the American College of Nutrition.* 28 Suppl. 500S-516S.

- Wilson, L. *et al.* (1901): *Egyptian literature. Egyptian Tales, Hymns, Litanies, Invocations, The Book of The Dead and Cuneiform Writings.* The Colonial Press.

Chapter 3

- Cardozo-Freeman, I. (1978): "Serpent Fears and Religious Motifs among Mexican Women". *Frontiers: A Journal of Women Studies*, 3 (3), 10-13.

- Cartwright, M. (2017). "Silk in Antiquity". https://www.worldhistory.org/Silk/

- Cartwright, M. (2019). "Yurt". https://www.worldhistory.org/Yurt/

- Cattermole-Tally, F. (1995): "The Intrusion of Animals into the Human Body: Fantasy and Reality". *Folklore,* 106: 89-92.

- Fletcher, J. (1994): "A tale of wigs, hair and lice", *Egyptian Archaeology* 5. 31-33.

- Fletcher, J. and Salamone, F. (2016): An Ancient Egyptian Wig: "Construction and Reconstruction", *Internet Archaeology* 42.

- National Park Service. (2015): "Caribou Skin Tents". https://www.nps.gov/gaar/learn/historyculture/caribou-skin-tents-1.htm

- Pauls, P. E. (2006). "Tepee". https://www.britannica.com/technology/tepee

- Pedrosa, J.M., Rubio Marcos, E. y Palacios, C.J. (2007): *Creencias y supersticiones populares de la provincia de Burgos. El cielo. La Tierra. El fuego. El agua. Los animales.* Colección Tentenublo, vol. 3.

- Silver, C. (2020): "Hair, Gender, and Social Status in Ancient Egypt". *JSTOR Daily.* https://daily.jstor.org/hair-gender-and-social-status-in-ancient-egypt/

- Stünkel, I. (2015): "The upside-down Catfish". The Met. https://www.metmuseum.org/blogs/now-at-the-met/2015/upside-down-catfish

- Verma, M. (2000): *Fasts & Festivals of India.* Diamond Pocket Books. New Delhi.

- CAMEO (2020): "Murex purple". http://cameo.mfa.org/wiki/Murex_purple

- https://museoecologiahumana.org/en/obras/bladder-bagpipes-pigs-bladder-elder-wood-thread/

- Museo Virtual de Ecología Humana (2021): "Bladder bagpipes". https://museoecologiahumana.org/en/obras/bladder-bagpipes-pigs-bladder-elder-wood-thread/

Part II: Rebirth

- Smarter Business (2020): Top Industries with the Highest Water Consumption. https://smarterbusiness.co.uk/blogs/the-top-5-industries-that-consume-the-most-water/

Have your veg and eat it

- Barilla Centre for Food and Nutrition (2021): https://food-sustainability.eiu.com/

- Organic Trade Association (2021): https://ota.com/organic-101/how-are-animals-raised-organically "How are animals raised organically?"

- Shurtleff, W. & Akiko Aoyagi (2014): *History of Meat Alternatives*. SoyInfo Center, California. https://www.soyinfocenter.com/pdf/179/MAL.pdf

- Soil Association (2021). https://www.soilassociation.org

- The Good Food Institute (2021): "Science". https://gfi.org/science/

No time to waste

- Astoria Journal (2021). "The Recycling Journey". Infographic. https://astoriajournal.com/wp-content/uploads/2021/01/Bottle-recycling.jpg

- Ellen MacArthur Foundation (2020): Upstream innovation: a guide to packaging solutions. https://plastics.ellenmacarthurfoundation.org/upstream

- Girón, S. (2021). "Spain's untapped 'liquid gold'". https://www.bbc.com/travel/article/20211014-spains-untapped-liquid-gold

- Hellmann's (2021): "The Plastics Problem". https://www.hellmanns.com/us/es/the-plastics-problem.html

- Johnson, J. (2019): "How to reduce food waste". Medical News Today. https://www.medicalnewstoday.com/articles/327325?c=160548707047

- Kubala, J. (2017): "20 Easy Ways to Reduce Your Food Waste". https://www.healthline.com/nutrition/reduce-food-waste

- Lin, F., *et al.* "Plant leaves for wrapping zongzi in China: an ethnobotanical study". *J Ethnobiology Ethnomedicine* 15, 63 (2019). https://doi.org/10.1186/s13002-019-0339-7

- Mustafa, M. *et al.* (2012). "Looking back to the past: revival of traditional food packaging". Conference: 2nd Regional Conference on Local Knowledge (Kearifan Tempatan), 15-16 October 2012

Building a future

- Badawy, A. (1958): "Architectural provision against heat in the Orient". *Journal of Near Eastern Studies,* 17, pp. 122-128.

- Davies, N. (1929): "The town house in ancient Egypt". *Metropolitan Museum Studies,* 1(2) pp. 233-255.

- Duckworth, C. N. and Wilson, A. (2020): *Recycling and Reuse in the Roman Economy.* Oxford University Press.

- Stouhi, D. (2017): "What is a Traditional Windcatcher?". *ArchDaily* https://www.archdaily.com/971216/what-is-a-traditional-windcatcher

- Wainwright, M. (2011): "Bricks made from sewage - Yorkshire's latest gift to the world". *The Guardian.* https://www.theguardian.com/global/the-northerner/2011/sep/15/yorkshire-water-leeds-university-sewage

- Watson, J. (2020): *How to build a resilient future using ancient wisdom.* TED2020. https://www.ted.com/talks/julia_watson_how_to_build_a_resilient_future_using_ancient_wisdom

Dressed for success

- Mogavero, T. (2020): Clothed in Conservation: Fashion & Water https://sustainablecampus.fsu.edu/blog/clothed-conservation-fashion-water

- The Conscious Challenge (2019): "Water and Clothing". https://www.theconsciouschallenge.org/ecologicalfootprint-bibleoverview/water-clothing

Closing the organic cycle

- Banks, I. *et al.* "Growth rates of black soldier fly larvae fed on fresh human faeces and their implication for improving sanitation". Tropical Medicine and International Health. Vol. 19, issue 1, Jan. 2014, 14-22

- Boztas, S. (2016): "Poo power: Dutch dairy industry launches €150m biogas project". *The Guardian.* https://www.theguardian.com/sustainable-business/2016/nov/02/netherlands-europe-dairy-industry-agriculture-biogas-cows-manure-poo-power

- Cormier, Z. (2017). "It's not a load of crap: turn your urine and faeces into treasure". *The Guardian.* https://www.theguardian.com/commentisfree/2017/aug/25/not-crap-turn-faeces-urine-treasure-astronauts-recycle-bodily-waste

- Davis, N. (2017): "Space savers: astronaut urine could make supplies from nutrients to tools". *The Guardian.* https://www.theguardian.com/science/2017/aug/22/srecycled-astronaut-urine-could-make-nutrients-and-tools

- Ellen MacArthur Foundation (2021): "What is a circular economy?". https://ellenmacarthurfoundation.org/topics/circular-economy-introduction/overview

- Fleming, N. (2018): "From stools to fuels: the street lamp that runs on dog do". *The Guardian.* https://www.theguardian.com/environment/2018/jan/01/stools-to-fuels-street-lamp-runs-on-dog-poo-bio-energy-waste-
- Richman-Abdou, K. (2019): "Kintsugi: The Centuries-Old Art of Repairing Broken Pottery with Gold". *My Modern Met.* https://mymodernmet.com/kintsugi-kintsukuroi/

Video resources:

- This London insect farm is changing the way we eat | Pioneers for Our Planet
- https://www.youtube.com/watch?v=zKvXtUHyZZ0
- Recycling revolutionary Veena Sahajwalla turns old clothes into kitchen tiles | Australian Story
- https://www.youtube.com/watch?v=4fkbQynfSyY
- Green buildings are more than brick and mortar | Bryn Davidson | TEDxRenfrewCollingwood
- https://www.youtube.com/watch?v=JEUShQ7r_tE&t=262s
- How Mushrooms Are Turned Into Bacon And Styrofoam | World Wide Waste
- https://www.youtube.com/watch?v=uznXI8wrdag
- Harie A Community Centered on Water
- https://www.youtube.com/watch?v=dYKVUbB8Ok8

Links to objects mentioned in order of appearance:

- The Turin Egyptian Museum's unique collection of ancient Egyptian organic remains, from textile to bread, is visitable virtually here: https://virtualtour.museoegizio.it/

135

- Model of a house: https://www.metmuseum.org/art/collection/search/544249

- Ovoid shape strainer jar: https://www.brooklynmuseum.org/opencollection/objects/21099

- Model of a sieve (and other cooking miniatures in different registers): https://www.liverpoolmuseums.org.uk/artifact/model-of-sieve-0

- Large Oval Storage Basket: https://www.metmuseum.org/art/collection/search/545131

- Egyptian broom: https://www.brooklynmuseum.org/opencollection/objects/118434

- Tarkhan dress: https://www.ucl.ac.uk/culture/petrie-museum/tarkhan-dress

- Rag ball: https://museums.bristol.gov.uk/details.php?irn=84473

- Relief of Queen Neferu Having Her Hair Done: https://www.metmuseum.org/art/collection/search/591390

- Bundle of hair extensions: https://www.brooklynmuseum.org/opencollection/objects/186373

- Fish rattle: https://www.brooklynmuseum.org/opencollection/objects/3520

About the author

María Correas-Amador holds a PhD in Archaeology from Durham University. Her field of specialism is organic architecture and ethnoarchaeology. She has carried out extensive fieldwork in Egypt, as well as being a university lecturer and a museum guide. She currently works as a translator, focusing on the field of sustainability and education.

María is also a co-founder of El Arpa, an initiative showcasing culture and art through events, articles and a podcast (People Will Talk).

Printed in Great Britain
by Amazon

83491815R00089